Scotland
Coast to Co

Scotland
Coast to Coast

A long distance walk from Glen Shiel to
Arbroath

Hamish Brown

Patrick Stephens Limited

First published in 1990

British Library Cataloguing in Publication Data
Brown, Hamish M., 1934–
   Scotland coast to coast: a long distance walk from Glen Shiel to Abroath: Kintail, Lochaber, Rannoch, Atholl, Angus.
1. Scotland. Recreations, walking visitors guides
I. Title
796.5'1'09411
ISBN 1–85260–229–5

Patrick Stephens Limited is part of the Thorsons Publishing Group, Wellingborough, Northamptonshire NN8 2RQ, England.

Printed by Woolnough Bookbinding Limited, Irthlingborough, Northamptonshire

10 9 8 7 6 5 4 3 2 1

Dedication

For Tony who has walked across Scotland with me four times on the Ultimate Challenge, and for Val and Livia who walked across on this particular route on UC 88.

There is nothing quite like a self-elected, self-selected, self-directed journey for ensuring an interesting journey. Such a stravaig appeals to the goat in us. The sheep simply follow. The sane and rational stay at home.

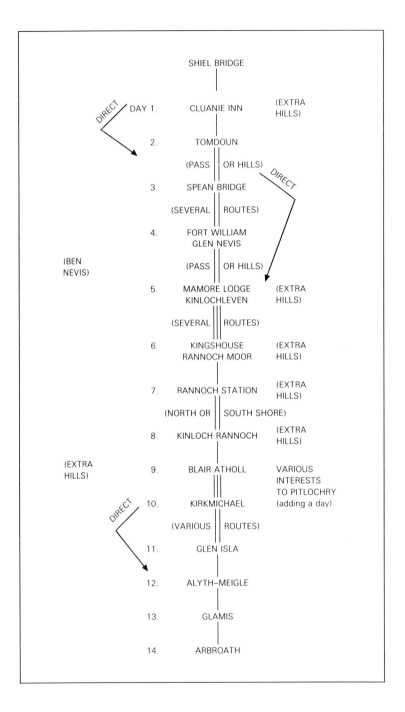

SHIEL BRIDGE

DIRECT DAY 1. CLUANIE INN (EXTRA HILLS)

2. TOMDOUN

(PASS   OR HILLS)   *DIRECT*

3. SPEAN BRIDGE

(SEVERAL   ROUTES)

4. FORT WILLIAM
GLEN NEVIS

(BEN NEVIS)

(PASS   OR HILLS)

5. MAMORE LODGE   (EXTRA
KINLOCHLEVEN   HILLS)

(SEVERAL   ROUTES)

6. KINGSHOUSE   (EXTRA
RANNOCH MOOR   HILLS)

7. RANNOCH STATION   (EXTRA HILLS)

(NORTH OR   SOUTH SHORE)

8. KINLOCH RANNOCH   (EXTRA HILLS)

(EXTRA HILLS)

9. BLAIR ATHOLL   VARIOUS
INTERESTS
TO PITLOCHRY

DIRECT 10. KIRKMICHAEL   (adding a day)

(VARIOUS   ROUTES)

11. GLEN ISLA

12. ALYTH–MEIGLE

13. GLAMIS

14. ARBROATH

Contents

Introduction

Regions mountainous and wild, thinly inhabited, and little cultivated, make a great part of the earth, and he that has never seen them, must live unacquainted with much of the face of nature, and with one of the great scenes of human existence.

Dr Samuel Johnson

The learned Doctor Johnson, an unfit Londoner in his sixties, made one of the first great exploratory journeys through the Highlands in the years that followed the events of the Forty-Five. Maps, and ideas, had hardly progressed beyond the 'here be dragons' state. Landscape itself was an enemy when it was such a wild country as the Highlands. Dr Johnson saw it as such but from the quotation above and the tenor of his book, published in 1785, we begin to feel a shift in attitudes. He marvelled. And we are the heirs of this discovery. We journey with far greater freedom but I trust that we marvel as well, that we make that practical 'comparison with reality'. Here is Dr Johnson's resonant picture of the Highlands.

'They [the hills] exhibit very little variety; being almost wholly covered with dark heath, and even that seems to be checked in its growth. What is not heath is nakedness, a little diversified now and then by a stream rushing down the steep. An eye accustomed to flowery pastures and waving harvests is astonished and repelled by this wide extent of hopeless sterility. The appearance is that of matter incapable of form or usefulness, dismissed by nature from her care and disinherited of her favours, left in its original elemental state, or quickened only with one sullen power of useless vegetation.

'It will very readily occur, that this uniformity of barrenness can afford very little amusement to the traveller, that it is easy to sit at home and conceive rocks and heath, and water-falls; and that these journeys are useless labours, which neither impregnate the imagination, nor enlarge the understanding. It is true that of far the greater part of things we must content ourselves with such knowledge as description may exhibit, or analogy supply: but it is true likewise, that these ideas are always incomplete, and that at least, till we have compared them with realities, we do not know them to be just'

Walking across Scotland from coast-to-coast is simply fun, so needs no justification, but such journey offers a complex of pleasures resulting from a mixture of challenge and self-indulgence, of freedom and discipline, of many little agonies and ecstasies; it is an intensely personal yet sociable activity, with as many motives, methods and rewards as there are people involved. Such a walk takes one to the grass roots, if not the bare bones, of the country. It gives an endlessly varying cross-section of Scotland, its scenery, wildlife, history and present situation. The distance involved is enough to make the crossing physically demanding and there is plenty of mental stimulus. The person who paddles in the eastern sea at the end of the coast-to-coast has made a journey in self-discovery and will be fitter, happier and less-cluttered than the same person about to depart the western seaboard. Good adventuring is not found only in the far corners of the world, thank God.

Every year, for the last twelve years, I have walked across Scotland — besides making many other extended backpacking trips over a busy lifetime in the Scottish hills. There is no better way one can come to know a country than by tramping it on foot but such tramps are usually the better for a certain framework or objective, which gives a discipline and form to what could be a vague venture. There are times when that discipline is needed, but don't let discipline blister into slavery. If the weather is obviously violent and going to stay that way for days then there is no merit in slogging the days away in wet misery. Go home and come again under sunnier conditions. This is not a race either: better to take the extra days exploring the byways and split the crossing over two visits than simply tear across in the minimal time possible. The route is hard enough that a few days *not* heading east are welcomed. As a friend once said, not altogether as a joke I suspect, 'The walking is all right but the rests are better!'

Picking a route to allow the comforts of sure accommodation each night has not been easy. There are huge areas, on both sides of Loch Ness or in the Cairngorms for instance, where overnight stops would have to be in tent or bothy. There is no accommodation and, very often, there are no local residents either. The scale and the emptiness of the Highlands can be frightening to the newcomer. This described route was teased out, over many years really, and then, in May 1988, I walked it throughout with two friends, as part of the Ultimate Challenge event.

That event was my brainchild and as it will no doubt be mentioned again I'll give a brief description here. It was a natural evolution from early explorations when I had to 'bike-n-hike' and came to know Scotland from long expeditions. Every schoolboy holiday was spent roaming Scotland and, later, as a teacher in what would become Outdoor Education, I had a decade taking youngsters into the wilds. I realized just how much that way of exploring Scotland meant to me when I was writing about those early days and, like most enthusiasts who naturally want to share their enthusiasms, I began to wonder how I could encourage others to go on longer tramps across country. The Ultimate Challenge was the outcome.

The event is not competitive. Participants choose their own route, tackle the crossing in their own style and may go alone or in a small party. Rules as such are kept to a minimum. Numbers are limited so there is a ballot, with 100 previous challengers and 100 newcomers being drawn, and 50 places being kept at the discretion of the organizers. About 200 usually make it, coast-to-coast, come sun or rain, and there have been more sunny crossings than wet ones. Spread over two weeks, and the bracketing weekends, this is just the right length of time for a crossing. It is never easy; but it is fun.

The Ultimate Challenge starts near the middle of May each

year, so some people who cannot obtain holidays then are apt to complain. Some will lose out, whatever the dates and, after all, there is no closed season for walking across Scotland. One can walk across in either direction of course but 'old hands' will usually opt for west–east as this goes with the prevailing winds and weather which can make quite a difference psychologically when conditions turn wild.

Some people (I'm not one I hasten to add) do like to have the luxuries of hot water and meals and a comfy bed each night but have found it difficult to design a route with such provisions. These various points have led me to work away at trying to have such a route and this book is the result: a route across Scotland that has a bit of everything, both walking, and in the evenings afterwards. The impecunious could still follow the route with the option of camping most nights. I have tried to strike a balance and have largely described the good places I've encountered, at reasonable prices, rather than the more expensive. Good food is more important I feel than the presence of a google-google box.

Obviously in a place like Spean Bridge, with a score of accommodation choices (or Pitlochry with a hundred) I cannot have experienced all of them. Apart from Fort William, Pitlochry and Arbroath I have tried to list most places however and would be glad to hear of any new B&Bs or useful facilities along the route or, conversely, if one has ceased to operate. Guide-books like this, which try to be comprehensive, soon fall out of date in some details. The hills and glens may stay the same, the walking is the same, but a dreamed-of café disappearing can be a blow to a tired walker limping towards a salvation brew. Despite roaming Scotland constantly, I cannot cover the whole route every year so my own knowledge will soon be less than it is at present and information from users will be welcomed: each year I'll prepare a sheet of additional practical information which those planning the walk can send for (see p. 211). One of the joys of the Ultimate Challenge is the friendliness and helpfulness of all those taking part and I would like to think that those following this route will feel part of a happy tradition and want to pass on helpful information.

One of the desires behind the UC event was to see hill goers putting something back more directly into the

Highlands where so much pleasure is taken. Hordes travel up, weekend by weekend, car boots full of supermarket food, car tank full of cheapest home petrol, take their sport, and return home. Their contact with and contribution to Highland life is minimal. If you are walking for two weeks you will be shopping, you will be meeting local people, you will be *contributing* as well as receiving. There are people in remote glens who now look forward to the UC as one of the year's highlights. Why not encourage such journeys at other times as well?

Timing is important. While most of the route is on rights-of-way this is not always so and many rights-of-way were made into good paths by private landowners for stalking and other interests. In Scotland we have a marvellous freedom to roam but it depends on mutual understanding and co-operation. We are hardly showing gratitude if we stravaig at unhelpful times. On pages 101–103 I mention more on this topic but basically, from mid-August to the third week in October, estates will be shooting stags and many summits or off-route attractions are best avoided then. Read the text carefully and design a route which will not interfere with others' activities. We would hate our sport to be spoilt: stalking, however, is not just sport, but a vital part of the economic survival of people in the Highlands.

Midsummer, being the open season for humans as far as attacking midges are concerned, is not the best time for walking anyway. The weather is frequently wet or warm and humid. Spring and autumn are much more colourful and refreshing and usually provide better weather. April may produce its traditional showers but can also give golden sunshine. The summits in April may still require ice axes and winter-walking knowledge. May and June are good months but do avoid starting on the weekend nearest the middle of the month when the UC will be commencing and accommodation, Friday to Sunday, may be more difficult to find round Loch Duich/Shiel Bridge. The crucial bookings are Rannoch Station and Kingshouse (with limited accommodation) so your starting date may depend on the dates you can book for those isolated places on either side of Rannoch Moor. July is a crowded tourist month so accommodation would have to be booked in advance. September sees the crowds thin again, October can vary but is often like April in reverse. By the end of the month the fiery colours of autumn will be capped by the first snows on the mountain tops. November to March, the winter months, will see few places open and a crossing then is not really a practical proposition. Many facilities (B&Bs, castles, museums, etc) operate from Easter to the end of September or mid-October. This guide is written on the assumption that readers will be making a crossing in that period.

This guide is, I hope, different from most in its offering alternatives whenever possible. The slavish following of a linear route is something I'd hate to see developing. So readers will have to make choices at times. If you want every step indicated this coast-to-coast effort is not for you. It is not a 'Way'. It is not a footpath route even. Parts of it are untracked and wild. A certain confidence and the ability to navigate is essential. Having said that I'm a firm believer that most people have a well-developed desire to stay alive and won't readily overdo things or run into trouble. A certain uncertainty and challenge is no bad thing in a world where we are far too 'directed'. You cannot have wilderness without the wild.

The main route of this crossing is thoroughly described but the alternatives are described more briefly while the mountain possibilities are just outlined. Those climbing Munros or Corbetts on the way should be capable of such undertakings without needing guidance. The 'style' of the crossing should be a matter purely for personal choice: how fast or slow, how hard or easy, is entirely up to you. It should be enjoyable *at the time* as well as in retrospect!

The route described allows one to travel light for, on each night, a meal, bed and breakfast should be possible. If travelling alone some contact with a base partner is advisable so if you do go missing this will be known soon rather than later or too late. Don't overload yourself: you fight every ounce of the way. At the back I've listed all the items I carried on my crossing. It did not include six pairs of stockings! Waterproofs and first aid are vital items which, hopefully, will be unused. Foot comfort is probably the greatest priority. A mere blister could end the crossing (a great waste of time, effort and finances) yet how avoidable that is. Make sure footwear is comfortable before you start. Part of the problem is giving boots or trainers or whatever a valid test beforehand. Snags may not show up till after several days of this harder-than-usual backpacking. So carry a variety of plasters, pads, corn-rings, etc (Scholl's do a wide range). Take twice the quantity of Elastoplast you think you'll need. Stop for two or three good breaks during the day and, as well as brewing, remove boots and stockings and have a paddle. Pamper your feet. Believe me, an army marches on the soles of its feet. Cheering the stomach is merely an extra pleasure. Caring for feet is much more important.

Carrying the 1:50,000 map should be adequate but in a few places the larger scale of 1:25,000 could be useful and these are indicated. Use the 1:50,000 *Second Series* maps, not older ones. The appropriate OS sheet number is given at the start of each day's description. The sketch maps in this book give minimal detail and show the main alternatives only. Things like maps, film, spare clothes, some goodies, etc, can well be posted ahead so the entire stock for the crossing does not have to be carried all the way. Remember to include some packing and stamps for returning the items no longer wanted. Post to B&Bs to avoid the snag of half days or closing hours at Post Offices.

One of the pleasures of the Ultimate Challenge event is its lack of complicated rules. Rules are few. One is 'no dogs' (May is lambing time) and though this may be unenforceable for an independent coast-to-coast walker, I'd suggest a dog on this route is not fair on the dog, nor the owner, nor anyone else. There is hardly a day where a dog would not present problems or be most unwelcome to farmers and shepherds. I say this as a fanatic dog-owner but feel affection enough for my dog NOT to take him along. Try a two-legged friend instead!

Two people is probably the best number in a party. Solitary walkers are often presented with problems finding single rooms while three often means a pair and one single, someone again being in the odd-man-out situation. In some cases a shake-down bed may be added to a double room or there may be three beds in a room. These things are best clarified before setting off.

There is no reason why one should not camp at night but if

one has a tent and is self-sufficient a recommended route like this is not specifically necessary: however I've added brief notes on the camping possibilities in the accommodation sections. All sites are mentioned, for the rest there is the option of 'wild' camping, ie, choosing a pitch in the wilds, without any facilities like toilets or litter bins. Campers must ensure they leave no sign of their passing. If using bar/hotel facilities there will be toilets available and litter can be disposed of in bins. Wild camping is a privilege, not a right, and should not be abused, or up will go the *No Camping* notices. Camp discreetly: find some quiet corner out of sight of houses and roads. Use a tent with natural colours and not the colour-polluting offerings the touts are pushing these days. Don't light fires. If the weather is foul you'll be inside the tent anyway, if the weather is good a fire is uncalled for. Several serious moor fires have been caused by campers in the last few years.

I have tried to point out some of the interesting places or features on the route as a walk like this gains immensely when something of the history, wildlife and local lore can be woven into the experience. Curiosity, I trust, is part of every walker's make-up. 'When you stop saying ''Why?'' You have started to die' has an element of truth in it. I've also touched on odd topics, like river crossings, in the text rather than here. The guide will not only be read beforehand to work out the practicalities of designing one's route but also day-by-day as the walk unfolds. So mentioning these things in context I think is better than too long an introduction. The walk does not stop on arrival at the next B&B. Thought and study needs to be given to the day ahead. Don't hesitate to ask local advice. Try to get a weather forecast. Plan accordingly. You are exploring country, not simply slicing through it.

One thing I've always tried to do is keep some record of my mountain doings. I always carry a smallish notebook and will keep a day-by-day log and will also stick in postcards or pictures from brochures or my own photographs of the trip — a very personal souvenir of such a crossing. You can list flora and fauna, add sketches or all manner of things. Do it for fun, at the time, and it will provide pleasures for decades to come. Just a few words can preserve so much and, years later, the memories can flood back in a way quite impossible if nothing has been written down. Like the walking itself this day-by-day recording requires a certain discipline. Strange, is it not, how much the fun and pleasure of hill doings are interwoven with planning and discipline? Out of that balance comes the pecular satisfaction of a coast-to-coast walk. We may be unsure and unfit at the start. By the end we will possess the earth! Even the redoubtable Dr Johnson on his journey noted that 'mountaineers have an agility in climbing and descending distinct from strength and courage, and *attainable only by use.*' Our trouble is that we arrive at Arbroath fit and able only to return to the fleshy world of our normal lives. Johnson did not miss much nor go under any misapprehension. He told his readers 'Mountainous countries are not passed but with difficulty, not merely from the labour of climbing; for to climb is not always necessary: but because that which is not mountain is commonly bog, through which the way must be picked with caution. Where there are hills, there is much rain . . . .'

For the day's activity I have not given the distance and amount of climbing involved, nor a time. Time, I feel, is far too subjective a matter, and is something parties should be working out for themselves. As a rough guide you can allow 4.5 kilometres per hour and 10 metres per minute for climbing. Every walker should learn to make his own estimations and judgements.

At times I find I want a map covering a much wider area, either to work out a summit view or to visualize several days ahead. The Bartholomew 1:100,000 series can be useful for this and the walk is covered by sheets 48, 49, 50 and 51. You might find these worth taking on the crossing.

Reading and exploring go hand in hand and where I have found local titles of interest I've listed these after the *Accommodation* and other notes. Books of more general interest are in the appendix. A paperback or two along the way may be welcome. You could even try my good/bad habit of reading while walking along the less exciting stretches of tarred roads.

There are few banks on the route and you may well arrive too late to use them, so it is advisable to carry a cheque book and/or adequate cash. It can be very frustrating trying to obtain money urgently — don't let it happen!

In some places (Cluanie, Tomdoun, Kingshouse, Rannoch Station) accommodation is very limited and a telephone booking beforehand is advisable. To battle across Rannoch Moor in a storm and find no beds at Rannoch Station is embarrassing to everyone! Where only one or two addresses are given this is, almost certainly, all there is in the way of accommodation. In more populous areas like Fort William or Pitlochry there are tourist offices open all year, in smaller places like Spean Bridge, Kinlochleven, Blair Atholl there is usually a Tourist Information Board listing facilities. If in doubt — ask!

Unless otherwise stated there should be no difficulty finding an evening meal but a packed lunch may not be so readily available and it is worth checking in advance. Stock up at towns and villages. Places like Tomdoun or Rannoch Station are simply lonely buildings many miles from any shop or other services. I'd always carry a stove and dixi, for picnic brews mainly, but a useful stand-by, as would be some general emergency rations.

This is *not* the sort of walk where you can fall out into a convenient chip shop, or pub, or catch a bus home. The line between sufficiency and desperate need can be a thin one on Rannoch Moor or beside a flooded Glen Loyne.

The biggest drawback of overnight accommodation as far as I'm concerned is that an early start is seldom possible but many of the places listed will co-operate and serve breakfast earlier than normal. You can render a service to all who follow by asking for early breakfast everywhere. Services are always the result of pressures being applied. If everyone asks for early breakfast, it will come! I cannot see why people want to waste half the morning before doing anything. The wildlife is at its best early. The weather is often better early.

> 'The walker gets his leaven
> In the hours before eleven.'

> 'Soak or sweat, off at seven
> Makes the day end in heaven.'

You may not be off at seven very often. But work on it!

In the first week of May the Scottish Six Day Trial takes

place: 300 motor bikes from all over the world charging about the mountains of Lochaber so, anywhere between Gleann Cia-aig and Rannoch Moor you may meet this 'hazard' or 'fascination', depending on how you view the sport. This premier British event has been going on since before the First World War so perhaps we should live and let live. Sadly, it has been won by foreign riders all through the 1980s.

The words Munro and Corbett will crop up frequently. For the uninitiated a Munro is a separate Scottish mountain over 3,000 feet (of which there are 277; compared to four in England) and a Corbett is a summit of 2,500 feet or more (with a clear 500 ft clearance all round, of which there are 221). They are named from Sir Hugh Munro, who listed all the peaks that bear his name, and J. Rooke Corbett (an Englishman) who both listed and climbed his now eponymous peaks. The Inaccessible Pinnacle baulked Munro several times and he died in France during the First War, with it and one he was keeping for last, still unclimbed. Thousands now find enjoyment (well, usually) in working through these lists but, be warned, Munroitis and Corbettitis are highly contagious diseases. There is no known cure. Coast-to-coast walking is perhaps the same — I know I've made twenty crossings! This book, I trust, will give the inspiration, not just to walk one, described, route, but to dream, design and do other crossings or big walks. Mountains can be horizontal as well as vertical. We may not make Everest but we can make fun.

Travelling up

When I have joined friends at Shiel Bridge for the start of coast-to-coast walks across Scotland there has been a certain irony in the travel to Shiel Bridge being easier and quicker for those starting in London than for myself, based in Fife, in the east of Scotland.

From London the overnight train journey to Glasgow and Fort William still has a certain romance to it. Whether in a sleeper or not one tends to wake to a view of high hills seen across long stretches of water (the Cobbler across Loch Long, Ben Lomond across Loch Lomond), the air is fresh and morning's feet patter in the corridors of expectation. The station names are a litany: Crianlarich, Tyndrum, Bridge of Orchy, Rannoch, Corrour, Tulloch, Roy Bridge, Spean Bridge, Fort William. From Rannoch Station one can cast speculative glances westwards over Rannoch Moor and eastwards to the cone of Schiehallion, this being the train's dissection of the walk: an emotive moment on what is still the most romantic railway route in Britain.

If the train gives a magic carpet journey (albeit an inimically dusty, worn, ancient carpet) Fort William brings you down to concrete. Fort William we will describe later, when it may be a welcome haven. Travelling up 'the Fort' is a functional junction; we just swop from train to bus, with perhaps a quick snack in Nevisport between. The train continues to sea-sounding Mallaig, which is another lure, the bus continues to Kyle and over the sea to Skye and Uig, the ferry port for the Outer Hebrides so, before you even start this journey, you will be dreaming of others. We abandon the bus where the Road to the Isles meets the western sea. Shiel Bridge. Loch Duich. Ratagan. Here are names to put in a glass and drink. The journey up is complete. The toast is to the walk ahead.

Timetables can vary and the winter and summer schedules change rather inconveniently in mid-May but basically there is the night train to Glasgow and the early morning continuation to Fort William. The departure from Glasgow is too early to make it possible to join the train there from all but the most local connections. I've got round this by going up to Crianlarich the night before and joining the train at about 7.30 am which is more reasonable. Crianlarich youth hostel is just below the station. Or you could travel on to most of the places named above and avoid early starting altogether. They all have local Bed and Breakfast facilities except Corrour (station bunkhouse, Ossian YH) and Tulloch (Fasgadh private hostel, 4 km). However you make, or break, the journey to Fort William, make sure of the bus to Shiel Bridge!

The bus comes from Glasgow as well, so travelling from there by bus is an option but the train journey is such a classic route that I'd recommend taking the train if possible. Another possibility is to travel via Inverness and the Kyle line, reaching Shiel Bridge by post-bus from Kyle of Lochalsh. The post-bus is only a Land Rover so cannot carry many passengers. There is also a bus service through to Kyle from Inverness — via the Great Glen (Loch Ness) and Glen Morriston. As you can make several different journeys to Shiel Bridge you will just have to come more than once. Next time though you can make an entirely personal journey, dreaming up your own route from Shiel Bridge to Valhalla, and putting feet to the dream.

With the vagaries of British travel the above is a bare outline of possibilities. You will have to do a certain amount of homework and below is a list of contacts which can help. If tempted to drive a car to the start remember the vehicle is going to sit unattended for two weeks and it could take a couple of days of trains/buses to travel back from finish to start. A car taken to Edinburgh or Glasgow and then garaged is one vehicle option worth considering.

Getting Around the Highlands and Islands is a

compendium of all timetables and an indispensable aid to planning. Available from FHG Publications, Abbey Mill Business Centre, Seedhill, Paisley PA1 1JN (041 887 0428) or from larger tourist offices, travel agents, bookshops, etc.

SYHA Handbook is essential if planning to use any hostels. The Scottish association's hostels are still used by walkers and are pleasanter than their bland English counterparts. Ratagan, Glen Nevis, Pitlochry are on the route.

Train travel: enquire locally or ring London, 01 262 3232; or Edinburgh Waverley, 031 556 2451; or Glasgow, 041 204 2844; or Fort William, 0397 3791.

Fort William bus station (next to the railway station) disgracefully has no office, so information from Glasgow, 041 332 9191 or 041 332 9644.

The _Fort William Tourist Office_ is 0397 3781 (open all year).

Some people consider walking the route is quite easy after all the planning and preparing and travelling that precedes the start. The journey up however is very much part of the adventure. Walking is simply the most superior form of travel.

The starting point: Shiel Bridge

OS33

Shiel Bridge is not a town but a straggle of houses and crofts where Glen Shiel reaches the western sea at Loch Duich. This clustering of people round such a site reflects the Clearances pattern when the glens were forcefully emptied of people to make way for the more profitable sheep. The glens of the north and west are empty to this day and bracken-covered piles of stones testify to that departed way of life. The sheep remain, even if their profitability has gone. The area is known as Kintail which is from Ceann, *head*, and means simply 'the head of the sea'.

There are several hamlets in fact which are loosely covered by the term Shiel Bridge. Shiel Bridge itself has 'the big house', Glensheil Lodge (Lord Burton), the camp site/shop/café/petrol/information office complex and a few houses. The A87 swings right (north) by the old croft houses of Invershiel to the Kintail Lodge Hotel, once the big house of the northern side of the glen. The north side of the glen contains the Five Sisters of Kintail, hills bought for the nation by Percy Unna and given to the National Trust for Scotland. A cutting leads through to Ault a' Chruinn and the modern causeway round to the north side of the loch under Corbett Sgurr an Airgid, passing Inverinate, a hamlet of forestry houses and on to Dornie, a busy, real village at the bridge over Loch Long and guarded by the much-photographed castle of Eilean Donan. At Ault a' Chruinn the original road breaks off to circuit round the marshy NE corner of Loch

THE START. Striding out: at the head of Loch Duich, Kintail Lodge Hotel and Sgur an Airgid behind.

Loch Duich, on the West Coast, the idyllic starting point of the walk.

Duich by Morvich where the National Trust for Scotland (NTS) have a visitor centre and camp site. From Shiel Bridge the original military road wends south of Loch Duich and then rears up over the Mam Ratagan.

A day at Shiel Bridge

Depending on transport there may be several hours or even a day available for explorations at Shiel Bridge, or you may want to take a day or two to climb some of the hills before heading off across Scotland. Below is a brief note of some of the things worth seeing and doing round the head of Loch Duich and about some of the hills in the area.

Eilean Donan Castle near Dornie is a bit far away but if a visit can be arranged it should not be missed. It was bombed by the navy in 1719 when held by Jacobite forces and lay ruined until this century when it was largely rebuilt (see p 34).

The Falls of Glomach are often claimed as the highest in Scotland but this is doubtful. The river plunges into a deep gorge in spectacular fashion anyway and some care is needed on its slopes. It is reached over the Bealach na Sroine and it would be possible to follow its river up to Loch a' Bhealaich and return over the Bealach an Sgairne, as demanding a round as climbing any hill. There is an interpretive display by the Morvich camp site and just along and across the A87 from the Kintail Lodge Hotel is the Museum of the Clan MacLennan with its enthusiastic custodian. At Ault a' Chruinn there is a restaurant, The Portbhan, and at Shiel Bridge the camp site shop also has a tea room. Try a ride up Mam Ratagan in the post-bus for its famous view and then walk down. The road along past the youth hostel towards Totaig is beautiful and little used by traffic. You could really spend all the holiday based on Shiel Bridge. Who wants to climb hills? Who wants to slog across Scotland?

The head of Loch Duich is ringed with peaks, all worthy of an ascent. Sgurr an Airgid can be climbed easily by the path up towards Beinn Bhuide and its East ridge. A' Ghlas-bheinn is a complex mountain which might be traversed by utilizing the paths over the Bealach an Sgairne ('The Gates of Affric') and the Bealach na Sroine. A path breaks off from the Bealach an Sgairne path to go up Coire an Sgairne which allows easy access to the vast plateau of Ben Attow. The Five Sisters of Kintail and The Saddle are in the super class: hills for the more experienced, with very long, steep slopes, some exposure and even scrambling. Sgurr Mhic Bharraich is a favourite hill of mine and has, several times, been the first hill climbed in a new year. The path by Loch Coire nan Crogachan is the normal approach. If we have to go off and walk across Scotland we could hardly start in a finer bit of the West than Kintail.

Accommodation: Shiel Bridge, Ratagan, Loch Duich

Bed and Breakfast

Mrs I. Campbell, Shiel House, Glenshiel, by Kyle of Lochalsh. 059 981 282.

Kintail Lodge Hotel, Glenshiel, by Kyle, Wester Ross, IV40 8HL. 059 981 275

Ratagan House Hotel, Ratagan, Glenshiel, by Kyle, Wester Ross, IV40 8HP. 059 981 272

Mrs H. Kerr, 5 Forestry Houses, Ratagan, Glenshiel, by Kyle, Wester Ross. 059 981 305

Mrs Sinclair, 8 Forestry Houses, Ratagan, Glenshiel, by Kyle, Wester Ross. 059 981 225

Mrs MacRae, Sgurr Fhuarain, Ratagan, Glenshiel, by Kyle, Wester Ross. 059 981 300

Mrs Mackinnon, Tigh-na-Mara, Altuchruine, Glenshiel, by Kyle, Wester Ross, IV40 8HN. 059 981 333

Mrs Campbell, Kishmul, Ratagan, Glenshiel, by Kyle, Wester Ross. 059 981 248

Ratagan Youth Hostel, Ratagan, Glenshiel, by Kyle, Wester Ross, IV40 8HT. 059 981 243

Mrs MacMillan, Achnagart, Glenshiel, Kyle, Ross-shire, IV40 8HU. 059 981 237 Offers B&B four miles up the glen on the morrow's route.

Inverinate B&B (059 981) 329; Dornie (059 985) 370, 357, 230, 293 are other B&B possibilities and Dornie has several hotels.

A' Ghlas–bheinn (left) and the long ridge of Beinn Fhada — the fine backcloth to Loch Duich, Kintail (the view from Mam Ratagan).

On the ridges of Kintail: the flat summit of Ben Attow.

Camping Sites are as indicated, at Shiel Bridge itself 937186, and at Morvich 961211. There is a shop and café at the former, the latter has a NTS visitor centre.

I've usually stayed in the hostel, having pleasant memories of it over many years; the hostel occupies a marvellous garden setting on the lochside ('between the Five Sisters and the setting sun') and has been tastefully modernized. Friends speak highly of Tigh-na-Mara (near the causeway). The Kintail Lodge is more up-market than anywhere else but a friendly welcome awaits you wherever you start. I hope you don't sleep well — you should be far too excited for that!

With the limited accommodation available at Cluanie Inn one alternative is to make Tomdoun in one day, crossing the South Kintail ridge, but this gives a 37 km day with 900 m of ascent, so is an option for the fit and competent. This route is outlined on p 36.

Glen Shiel

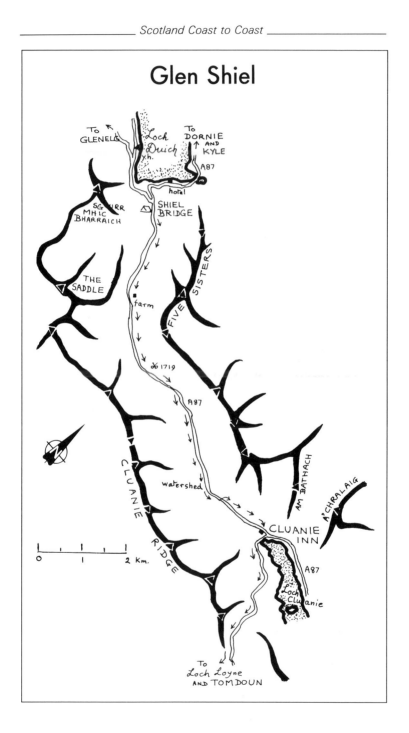

Day 1

Up Glen Shiel to Cluanie Inn

OS33

This is a varied and delightful walk for the busy A87 is avoided in favour of an ascent by the ever-changing River Shiel, a variation of the glen route I only tried after too many hard road trudges. Having gone up this 'wrong side' of the glen three times now, with different parties, I'm glad to say everyone agrees it is the best route possible.

Wherever one may be staying round Loch Duich the first job is to walk along to Shiel Bridge. This bridge was built by Thomas Telford so is pleasantly functional. The view from it up to the Five Sisters of Kintail is classic and the field to the west (on the south side) is lined with a row of seven splendid horse chestnut trees. Keep to the south side of the river, passing Glenshiel Lodge with its pale pink rhododendron screen and, crossing the Allt Undalain by an older bridge, reach the camp site/shop/café/petrol station/tourist office complex. Cross the River Shiel by the merely functional A87 bridge and immediately turn off it to begin the walk up past Loch Shiel.

Loch Shiel's capacity varies and the glen foot can flood in long periods of wet weather. The driest line is often up the banks a bit, following one of the many sheep tracks. In winter whooper swans often live on this small loch. Just past a ruin the track passes under a crag and is rather boggy but one can escape towards the river, through the alder trees, and walk up the river bank. The river flows deep and slow, tempting for a swim, but beware of skeleton trees below the surface. One

One of the many delightful falls encountered while walking up Glen
Shiel (east of the Telford Bridge).

Glensheil Lodge at Shiel Bridge.

decaying alder held a merganser nest we noticed last time. A succession of large, walled fields follow. These are often full of sheep and lambs in the spring so dogs should never be brought this way. A section of farm track is picked up but soon left again to simply wander across and up towards Achnangart, which is still a working croft (B&B, see under Shiel Bridge accommodation). A clump of pines grows by a field wall and if one aims for this a gate in the wall is seen. Go through this, making sure to secure the gate (and subsequent ones) and along above and parallel to the wall. Turn down to a gate in line with the farm and turn left once through it to another gate just left of the sheepfank which sits in the gap between a large knoll and the main hillside. There is a view from the gap of the river and the road curving up the glen. Above are the bold, steep flanks of the Five Sisters: one of the steepest and longest continuous slopes in Britain. On one dreadful day when I walked up it felt as if the whole flank was one enormous waterslide. The glen can be a fearsome place in conditions like that.

Conditions were seldom pleasant for the fugitive Bonnie Prince Charlie who hid for a while by a big boulder a mile on from Achnangart after he'd broken through the Redcoat cordon above Loch Hourn and crossed the south Glen Shiel hills by the Bealach Duibh Leac. Often wet and exhausted, dirty and ill-clad, sick and hungry, drunk and depressed the prince nevertheless covered a tremendous amount of rough country. Think of him if you find the next few miles a bit discomforting.

Perhaps this part is at its best in May. No doubt there will be the ubiquitous cuckoo calling, a sandpiper flickering up the river, a buzzard glinting among the crags. The trees are in new leaf and in secretive corners are primroses and wild hyacinths, wood sorrel and yellow pimpernel. A small gorge gives warning of the change from strath to glen and then it becomes altogether wilder, with crags falling steeply to the now noisy river and a route having to be teased along narrow ledges. The more timid may have to make diversionary ascents uphill but bits of animal track will lead on close to the river. You may be lucky and spot some of the feral goats: great shaggy beasts in brown-black colours, the big billies with sweeping horns.

Ahead, a knobbly hill can be seen in the middle of the glen, with the river tumbling down in a succession of waterfalls north of it and overlooked by wooded crags. Cross a small meadow to the foot of this gorge and pick a way up. There are no easy escape lines higher up and some care is needed in crossing jumbles of fallen boulders. It is more exciting than difficult. The setting is grand, in spate the din is tremendous and, looking out, the Forcan Ridge of the Saddle and the *whelk* of Faochag tower up. I'm almost certain it was this latter hill which called forth laudatory comment from Boswell when he and Dr Johnson came this way in 1773. The doctor slapped Boswell down by describing his 'immense' mountain as merely a 'considerable protuberance'.

Almost as a surprise the gorge relents and one looks along to the famous Telford Bridge which, until recent times, carried the A87 traffic. The grassy corners under its protective walls are good spots for a lunch break. Have an icy paddle while your stove brings the tea water to the boil. Relax and enjoy the tranquil scenes — which, in 1719, rang with the clash of battle.

Everyone knows of the Forty-Five, many know of the Fifteen, these being major Jacobite attempts to regain the throne, but few know about the rebellion of 1719 which more or less started and finished here in Glen Shiel. About thirty Spanish ships set sail for Scotland (a mini Spanish Armada) but only two reached the coast, sailing into Loch Duich and landing about 300 troops and the Jacobite leaders, the Earl Marischal, the Earl of Seaforth and the Marquis of Tullibardine. No more sails appeared but some other clansmen gathered, including Rob Roy and some MacGregors. The Jacobites moved up Glen Shiel and were met by General Wightman, the Scottish Commander-in-Chief who defeated them in a rather one-sided battle. The Highlanders dispersed and the poor Spanish lads were captured. A hill above the site is still Sgurr na Spainteach, *the peak of the Spaniards*.

Don't let the battle site take all your attention. Beyond the wooded knoll across the glen a burn comes down to join the River Shiel in a success of falls and tucked in below the A87's retaining wall is a water-worn gash with one lively fall, the Eas nan Arm. A few hundred yards up the A87 the first

The Telford Bridge near the 1719 battle site in Glen Shiel. The Saddle is the fine peak beyond.

stream coming down through the forest has a fall we always knew as the Serendipity Falls for it lay completely hidden just inside the trees, only to be discerned by pedestrians rather than the racing motorist. The trees, alas, have now been cut back to bring the falls to view. From there cut down to walk beside the River Shiel again — much more pleasant than the A87 verges.

The river bank can be followed for an hour or more. There are plenty of small falls and interesting corners. At one stage the river has cut into the bank and the damaged fence is a bit of an obstacle. A footbridge is passed and eventually one is more or less forced to take the A87 as road and river are crowded close and the banks are often rubble-covered. The road, at the narrowest part, has been reconstructed on the old river course and the waters are diverted through a tunnel. A steeper gradient leads to the glen's watershed and the road's highest point at 271 m.

Unfortunately the Old Military Road has been overwhelmed by forestry plantings but a mile further on, where a river drains the impressive corries to the north (a fine waterslide exits from Coire na Cadha), the forest stops and one can go through a gate on the east bank up to a sheep shelter and take to the line of the old road, a much safer route than along the modern road and the slight extra height yields very fine views of the Cluanie Ridge to the south. There are seven Munros on that sweeping, corrie-bitten, ridge-buttressed crest. An old deer fence comes down the hillside across the old road and later on a superbly-constructed circular sheep shelter is built on its line, but the route is clear enough and edged with a more modern fence for most of the way.

'At last', some may feel, the Cluanie Inn is suddenly in view and the old road drops to a gate on the last bend of the A87 before this historic travellers' haven which is, strictly speaking, not in Glen Shiel, but Glenmoriston.

Johnson and Boswell came from Invermoriston — a huge day to reach Glenelg — and somewhere along here they had a noonday halt. The idea of writing up his wanderings was born then:

'I sat down on a bank, such as a writer of Romance might have delighted to feign. I had indeed no trees to whisper over my head, but a clear rivulet streamed at my feet. The day was calm, the air soft, and all was rudeness, silence, and solitude. Before me, and on either side, were high hills, which by hindering the eye from ranging, forced the mind to find entertainment for itself. Whether I spent the hour well I know not; for here I first conceived the thought of this narration.'

Alternative start: Shiel Bridge to Tomdoun

As already mentioned this is an alternative for the strong hill walkers, but if Cluanie Inn is fully booked it is an interesting option, using a very historic pass. If 37 km, 900 m and wild country appeal it is worth considering anyway. Walk up the glen, as above, to Achnangart then cross the river to the A87 and along it for 1 km to the bridge over the Allt Mhalagain. The path for the Bealach Duibh Leac starts just east of the bridge.

The pull up is steep and steady. If you find it hard work think of the fugitive Prince crossing it in his wandering after Culloden. The Bealach Duibh Leac (*pass of the black slabs*) is 721 m, and feels it. The path drops steeply onto the balder, grassier south side of the Cluanie Ridge, to follow down

Cluanie Inn with the sprawl of A' Chralaig beyond.

Glen Shiel's deep trench from the ridge above it.

Wester Glen Quoich to Alltbeithe then climbs up again through Easter Glen Quoich to gain the valley of the River Loyne. This is magnificently wild country. Take the fork at 087060 to cross the river and traverse up to the Mam na Seilg pass for Tomdoun. On the subject of crossing the River Loyne and the continuation to Tomdoun refer to page 42, for this is also the route from Cluanie to Tomdoun.

Extra day(s) at Cluanie

The Cluanie Inn is a good base for the surrounding hills: Aonach Mheadhoin (not named, though the Munro, next to Sgurr an Fhuarail), Ciste Dhubh (seen up the Caorann Beag), Am Bathach (a Corbett with a special view), the mighty pair of A' Chralaig/Mullach Fraoch-choire, some of the Cluanie/South Kintail ridge to the south, all these are there for the keen hill walker, now or on some return visit.

Accommodation: Cluanie

The Cluanie Inn, Glenmoriston, Inverness-shire IV3 6YW, 0320 40238, is the only accommodation in the area so it is essential to book in advance. If full then a bus or hitch or taxi could be taken back down the glen for the night, returning next morning.

Another alternative for those who motored up with a partner planning to take the car home again is to keep the driver for this night. If the Cluanie is full he/she can run you down to Shiel Bridge for the night and back up again the next day to resume the walk.

Camping There are no sites but tents are often pitched beside the old road near the bridge at 077113. The western extension of the loch shown on the map is usually without water. If returning here at the end of the crossing one alternative is to camp and then leave the tent at the inn for collection later.

Reading Johnson, S.: *A Journey to the Western Isles*, 1785. (Reprinted in more recent years with notes by Finlay J. Macdonald: Macdonald, 1983.)

Day 2

South to Tomdoun

OS33, 34

This is one of the key days of the coast-to-coast and if the weather is diabolical (as it can be) one should seriously consider waiting a day or two before committing oneself to the crossing. There is a serious river crossing and the day takes the traveller through completely uninhabited country. Given reasonable conditions the feeling of splendid isolation and utter peace will leave a strong impression. Glen Loyne is worlds away from Piccadilly Circus!

From Cluanie Inn walk east along the A87 for 300 metres then turn off southwards on what is the original road from the south. The line of this old road can be seen rising across the

The start of day 2: Setting off from the Cluanie Inn (or walkers' tents) for the crossing to Tomdoun.

On the Cluanie Ridge. The view from Creag a'Mhaim to Druim Shionnach, Glen Shiel beyond, right.

Fording the River Loyne in easy conditions, the hill above is Creag a'Mhaim.

lower slopes of the hills and gives an easy tramp to start the day. The road now exists to serve Cluanie Lodge and at the junction with the lodge road there is a locked gate across the old road. There are good views northwards across Loch Cluanie to the A' Chralaig–Sgurr nan Conbhairean hills as one follows the bends up and round to the col between Creag a' Mhaim, the most easterly of the Cluanie Ridge Munros, and Beinn Loinne, the isolated Corbett which dominates the south shores of Loch Cluanie. Both are excellent viewpoints and worth an ascent but the Corbett lies beyond a very peat-boggy area and is more demanding than the higher Munro, which has a path all the way to its summit. Rather annoyingly this area is right on the edge of sheets 33 and 34 and it might be easier to use the 1:25,000 Pathfinder map no 237 *Loch Loyne*, though this map tends to live up to the series name with the vital paths difficult to find.

Just beyond the watershed and before the bridge over the Allt Giubhais is reached some decisions have to be made. The old road wends down eastwards to vanish into the waters of Loch Loyne and then rises to a col at 237 m before descending to Tomdoun. Just occasionally the loch level drops, after a long drought, so the drowned bridge surfaces and the road can be used to cross; but the situation should be ascertained through binoculars from a few hundred metres up the Creag a' Mhaim path rather than walking 5 km down the road only to find the loch impossible to cross.

The path up Creag a' Mhaim leaves the old road 100 m short of the bridge over the Allt Giubhais and wends upwards in determined fashion. After $\frac{1}{2}$ km it splits and the right fork continues to zig-zag right up to the summit of the Munro, 947 m, making it one of the easiest peaks of its size. The view is extensive in every direction. An easy walk of $1\frac{1}{2}$ km across a gentle saddle leads to a second Munro, Druim Shionnach, 987 m. The last pull to the summit is up a narrow, rocky crest, with wild corrie views down on either side. Such grandeur with such ease is not very often on offer in the Scottish hills but inexperienced walkers should only go high in settled, clear weather. The snow can linger long in the corries but the crests are usually clear. Dr Johnson, from the glen below, had an experience which is repeated for countless visitors now.

'Towards the summit of one [hill] there was a white spot, which I should have called a naked rock, but the guides, who had better eyes, and were acquainted with the phaenomena of the country, declared it to be snow. It had already lasted to the end of August, and was likely to maintain its contest with the sun, till it should be reinforced by winter.'

The left fork of the Creag a' Mhaim path crosses the saddle behind Creag Liathtais and angles down to Glen Loyne under the eye of the northern corries of Spidean Mialach. In wet conditions it is as well to use this path and then try to ford the River Loyne as soon as possible. There is a reasonable crossing where the stalkers' path heads up Spidean Mialach and a kilometre downstream another path crosses the Loyne and then rises to cross a pass to Glen Garry. Whatever is chosen this path and pass (the Mam na Seilg) is the ultimate objective. These wet-weather alternatives are mentioned first but, hopefully, they are a last resort. Certainly I've never had to use them, on each of three occasions making the straight crossing which is now described.

From the old road bridge over the Allt Giubhais simply follow down the banks of that stream into Glen Loyne. As the valley is reached there are some ruins and some perched boulders, a strange, sad place, utterly forsaken one feels. Follow the Giubhais down to the River Loyne and somewhere near the junction paddle across. A stark, dead tree downstream and a living tree upstream are good markers for this fordable stretch of the Loyne. A paddle may be quite welcome. On hot days I'll try to have several paddles and brews in the course of the day's walk. This is a marvellous place to have a break.

On river crossings

The River Loyne is our one serious river crossing but plenty of the glens, in the west especially, present similar problems. (Many are the epics of fact and story that come out of wet-year UC events!) It will do no harm to outline some of the practicalities of coping with such rivers. Never, ever, be rash: rivers in spate can kill so very easily. Dangerous spates are almost always the result of torrential rain and such rain is seldom of long duration. The water will subside as fast as it

The landmark tree at the Glen Loyne Crossing — and time for tea.

rose. Wait a few hours, camp overnight, go round, go back and try again later; these options are all better than drowning, yet people still do drown.

Most Highland rivers will be stony and/or slippery so wear your boots unless you have feet of leather. Socks can be taken off to keep them dry. Pack everything tidily into your rucksack (items dangling can upset your balance) and loosen straps so if you do fall in you can escape from the rucksack (which can pin one down in a frightening fashion). Study the river, work out the route, and then cross without hurry and without dithering. Keep in balance and move smoothly.

Face upstream (so the force of water doesn't buckle you at the knees) and if you have a stick this is a very useful prop. If there are several of you, hang on to each other in a scrum for mutual support. Shuffle across slowly, taking short steps. Use protruding boulders with caution. They may have hollows beside them and they can increase the water force. If boulder-hopping is possible the first person will inevitably wet the rocks which can then be slippery for anyone else following. Never attempt leaps at the limit of one's capabilities. In a fast-flowing river I'd suggest *not* crossing if the water is approaching thigh depth. Drowning usually occurs when someone is swept away. Being able to swim will make little difference. Deep, still water is not a problem — in fact it is often an easy, safe alternative (as for the Loyne)

43

A red deer hind near Tomdoun, in summer: they calve in June. The mating 'rut' occurs in the autumn.

which I've never seen discussed in practical manuals.

Assuming you can swim, such deep stretches of river or the outflow into a loch, are relatively safe places to cross. A swim may or may not be very pleasurable, depending on the temperature, but it is preferable to drowning! Place everything in your (bright orange) bivy bag and knot the mouth, which not only keeps things dry but provides a fantastic buoyancy-aid. In the water this burden weighs nothing. One bag can easily take two people's gear. Thus, if the Loyne is in spate, one alternative is to go down to the end of Loch Loyne and swim an arc-like route across the inflow. There is no danger of being swept away to be battered and drowned. Our old friend Dr Johnson had his word on 'such capricious and temporary waters' as he called spates:

> 'We passed many rivers and rivulets, which commonly ran with a clear shallow stream over a hard pebbly bottom. These channels, which seem so much wider than the water that they convey would naturally require, are formed by the violence of wintry floods, produced by the accumulation of innumerable streams that fall in rainy weather from the hills, and bursting away with resistless impetuosity, make themselves a passage proportionate to their mass.'

After one crossing we decided to walk along south of Loch

Loyne to rejoin the old road where it emerges from the loch, this being the nearest line to the broken right-of-way. The going is diabolically rough, being untracked peat, and the Mam na Seilg route is preferable. This is an historic pass which appeared on the earliest maps in the 18th century but in the deer season it would be as well to check that stalking is not taking place near it. High-velocity rifles are even worse than a few miles of peat bog! The inconvenient waters of Loch Loyne, by the way, are fed by tunnel through to Loch Cluanie.

The Mam na Seilg path comes from the crossing further up the glen but can be joined by going straight over (boggy) and up the hill from our paddling spot. The gap and the path leading up to the pass can be seen clearly during the descent by the Allt Giubhais. The *pass of the hunt* is a satisfying gap and the view southwards, suddenly revealed, has a richness to it compared to the bleak tawny sweeps of Glen Loyne with its ruins and remnants of forest. The path descends steadily (2 km) to reach the quiet Glengarry–Kinloch Hourn road at the bridge over the Allt a' Ghobhainn. Tomdoun Hotel lies $4\frac{1}{2}$ km along the road, eastwards. I've seen us glad to indulge in another paddle and brew before tackling that tarmac finish.

Accommodation: Glengarry/Tomdoun

Tomdoun Hotel, By Invergarry, Inverness-shire, 08092 218, is another old inn which, if it has lost its ancient 'Road to the Isles' trade is now a great favourite with fishermen and walkers. The accommodation ranges from the luxurious to bunkhouse to bothy and the food is both excellent and served in quantity. The only other B&B is Ardochy Lodge Guest House, $5\frac{1}{2}$ km to the east, beyond the Greenfield junction. There is nothing westwards from Tomdoun.

Camping Wild sites near the hotel are possible; ask at the hotel for advice.

Reading Ellice E. C.: *Place Names of Glen Garry and Glenquoich*, Routledge, 1931.

Tomdoun–Spean Bridge

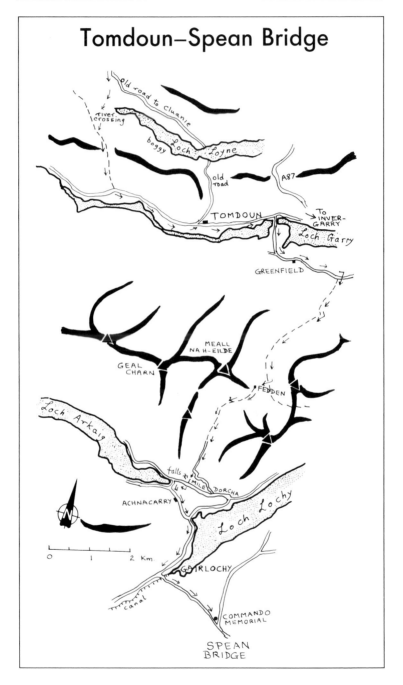

Day 3

To Spean Bridge and the Great Glen

OS34

This is a long and varied day even by the easiest of the routes offered here and there is no possibility of cutting corners. (One alternative, however, would be to follow along the south side of Loch Garry to the hamlet of Invergarry, overnight there — hotel, B&Bs, youth hostel, etc — and follow down the west side of Loch Lochy to rejoin today's route at Clunes — a longer route but done over two days.) The hardier walker can turn today into a magnificent expedition by taking in some of the summits lying south of Loch Garry. The 'straightforward' walk is described first.

A. The hill pass route

Set off east from Tomdoun, along the main road — if that is how you could describe the quiet road that runs from the Great Glen to the remote *fjord* of Loch Hourn. The road wends along through pleasant woodland but open enough to the south to give continuous views to the hills that have to be crossed. Ben Tee, to the east, is an unmistakable pyramid shape, one of those instantly recognizable hills which stand out from many directions. Inchlaggan is passed, a small forestry hamlet (no facilities). When the Greenfield bridge appears one can cut down to walk the lochside sheep tracks to reach it. This is the bridge which is so well seen from the sweep of the A87 as it pulls up from the Garry, foreground to one of the finest roadside panoramas in the country.

Greenfield lies 1½ km to the south, an oasis in the sea of conifers. One of the possible hill days starts here (see p 55). The forestry road pulls up and along eastwards for 3 km to the Allt Ladaidh (*laddie* is the pronunciation). Keepers once showed me names scribbled on the inside walls of the hut — from over 100 years ago. Take the track up the east bank of the Allt Ladaidh but, beware, Glengarry Forest is now a forest of trees, not deer ground. Vast extra areas are planted and the path shown branching off the Allt Bealach Easain path has been wantonly ploughed over and planted, despite being a right-of-way. One is forced to go half way up to the Bealach Easain to follow along outside the forest fence, a messy alternative, especially if the Six Day Trials have gone through recently. Regain the original track beyond the plantation. This swings south through a bald glen between bold hills to pass along above Lochan Fhudair. The loch is shown as having an exit at both ends. There is an old story of someone living nearby who, whenever he heard of the rent-man approaching, would quickly divert his local stream to flow on the appropriate side of the house so he could claim not to be liable, the stream being the boundary between Cameron and Glengarry lands. When the path begins to rise leave it to drop down over to the ruin of Fedden where another path is joined. It runs under the extremely steep cone of Meall an Tagraidh then angles down to reach the Abhainn Cia-aig at a bridge which you may or may not feel brave enough to cross (it has seen better days) but normally the river can be crossed by boulder-hopping just downstream. The path continues along the east bank of the river to reach the start of a large forest. There is a stile and the path continues clearly down through the trees before giving a sudden sharp rise (unwelcome to hot, tired walkers) to join the end of a proper forestry road.

As many of the mature trees have been felled there are some excellent views to the chunky cliffs of Ben Nevis,

---

Top left *Setting out from Tomdoun, Sgurr Gairich is the peak behind.*

Above left *Heading across the Greenfield Bridge in Glen Garry.*

Left *Loch Garry — the pass to Gleann Cia–aig heads between the two hills.*

straight ahead as one walks down the road. A locked gate across the road is reached but there is a stile beside it. Shortly after, a cairn by the roadside indicates where a steep path plunges down through the woods. As this keeps close to the edge of the Chia-aig gorge its use is discouraged — it is fenced off for those walking up from the road — and it is certainly steep, rough and unkept. The official path down through the forest lies some 300 m further on and is clearly indicated. It is a better made path. The path comes out at the Eas Chia-aig, a double-leap falling into a cauldron pool, a delightful fall, best seen from the road bridge. There is a small car park. This road runs west to the end of Loch Arkaig so sees little traffic.

Heading eastwards the initial stretch of road is known as the Mile Dorcha (*the Dark Mile*) a name best know as the title of the last book in D. K. Broster's Jacobite trilogy which has much of its action set in this Clan Cameron country. Older maps I recall marked a Prince Charlie's cave up on the crags north of here but they are so planted over that few can know its exact location now. The prince was in hiding there 15–17 August 1746.

The Mile Dorcha to Clunes has a sombre atmosphere but the walk by Bunarkaig has some beautiful spots with Ben Nevis often seen across Loch Lochy. However, this is very much a dog-leg of a route and pedestrians (not motorists) can walk through more directly by Achnacarry. Turn west from the Cia-aig car park, then left at the private road that skirts the end of Loch Arkaig. Across the rattling bridge turn left again and Achnacarry is soon reached. There are some magnificent trees on the road. Keep to the road please. The big house, glimpsed to the left, is the seat of the Cameron Chief, Lochiel. If he is at home his standard will be flying above the house.

'Gentle Lochiel' of the Forty-Five suffered for joining his Prince and Achnacarry was burned in the bloody aftermath of Culloden. He is reputed to have been planting trees when the news came of the Prince's landing. The saplings were quickly 'schooched-in' but survived and grew into great trees. Lochiel went off, rather reluctantly, and his casting in his lot for the Prince probably ensured the rash venture went forward.

Not all the Camerons were 'gentle'. A Cromwellian force building a fort was attacked by Sir Ewan Cameron of Lochiel and in the fray Ewan and a big soldier engaged in single combat. When the soldier was disarmed he leapt on the Cameron and they rolled down a bank in a desperate tussle. The soldier reached for his dagger and Ewan, in desperation, sank his teeth in the man's throat. Legend adds a sequel to this bloody bit of history. Lochiel was in London many years later and, at the barber's, his Scots accent was recognized. Lochiel asked if the barber knew anyone from Scotland. The barber replied, 'No, nor do I wish to, unless it was to have under my hands the fellow who bit the throat out of my father'.

Achnacarry was rebuilt when the forfeited estates were returned late in the 18th century but it was accidentally burned again during the Second War when the house was used for Commando training and other special, and often secret, courses. If you consider life hard, just think of the Commandos out on their survival courses in these hills, with no real shelter and only the food they could find. A young Commando, half-starved, found his Sergeant cooking some animal wrapped in clay in the embers of a fire. When the covering was opened the smell was delicious and the youngster begged a bite. The Sergeant generously shared his meal. 'And what was that?' came the question as fingers were licked at the end of the meal. 'That, sonny, was a rat.'

The road wanders on past a small post office with a flowery garden and several estate houses to eventually rejoin the public motor road at the SW corner of Bunarkaig Bay. Follow this along and then down to Gairlochy, the locks on the Caledonian Canal. There are some splendid trees on this bit of road. There are no facilities at Gairlochy: just the two sets of locks and the original houses. The canal was opened in 1822 and is justly famous. Its creator, Thomas Telford, did much else in the Highlands with almost 1,600 km of road, 1,200 bridges and about thirty churches and manses to his credit. The Caledonian Canal is his greatest monument. He sometimes had to invent new techniques and even design new machines or tools to cope with the challenging task. He must have been a remarkable man for he brought together highly talented experts some of whom stayed with him for decades. Everyone thought highly of Telford. The son of a Dumfriesshire shepherd he began life as a humble mason but was driven by a fanatic urge to make good — and to make good works — a workaholic, a perfectionist, yet apparently a man who was respected and liked by everyone, an engineer who enjoyed poetry.

The original lock-keeper's house lies beside the locks. Telford himself was based there periodically and the present lock-keeper can trace his family back to those first days — several generations of canal employees. Canals are like that and the Caledonian Canal is the most romantic in Britain. Walking down by the canal is one option for reaching Fort William (see B page 60).

The road swings round by an ancient graveyard and on alongside the wide, dark, River Spean. In the fields to the left Viscount Dundee gathered the clans for the Stewart king in 1689 — a story that ended at Killiecrankie, which we pass in a few days' time. The next interesting place is the Bridge of Mucomir, which was built by Telford to channel the River Lochy into the River Spean when the canal was being constructed. There is now a small hydro-electric generating station making use of the difference in height of Lochy and Spean. Shortly, to the right, is a camping and caravan park built on the site of the old Gairlochy Station on the Fort Augustus railway route. This line opened in 1903 and was never really financially viable so it was closed down in 1946. The linear shape of the site is explained by the previous use of the area!

The road pulls up steeply and passes the plain white building of the Free Church which was built after the Disruption of 1843. The Disruption was a mass exodus of the Church of Scotland in a refusal to accept the continuance of patronage: a courageous moral event for the ministers were, at once, homeless and churchless and often the landowners opposed the building of new 'Free' churches. In one case the locals had to worship in a floating ark.

Look back, down to the Spean, just before the highest point on the road (108 m). There is a car park view point. The road bends right, then left, this wiggle marking the place where Wade's road is crossed. After the bend right there is a gate, on the same line, and Wade's road can be seen running

Above _The Great Glen — the Caledonian Canal at Gairlochy with the Aonachs beyond._

Right _Gairlochy locks — the_ Eye of the Wind _passing through the Caledonian Canal._

down towards the River Spean. Neither it, nor the course of
the old railway from the Gairlochy camp site, are
recommended routes. The bridges over the mighty Spean
have gone and the walking is very wet. For once, the road is
best. One legitimate diversion if heading for the small, quiet
camp site at Stronaba, is to follow Wade's road north
through the trees. The line of the road has been partly lost in
the plantings but there is a large ride on the line of the power
line. (Gate opposite the 108 car park.) A third camp site lies
at Moy Farm, 2 km, along the canal (or B8004) towards
Banavie. One of Telford's original 'accommodation' bridges
still crosses the canal to the farm fields beyond.

The walk along to the Commando Memorial offers
sweeping views of Ben Nevis and the three other 4,000 ft
summits. The stark, simple and effective memorial was
unveiled in 1952 by the Queen Mother, the work of Scott
Sutherland, and is always popular with passing motorists. To
stand there alone, as we walkers can, in the quiet of evening
or in early morning, is to know an enriching experience.

B. Possible hill additions

Ben Tee is such a shapely cone that it is instantly
recognizable from anywhere around the Great Glen or along
the Garry. Its isolated situation makes it one of Scotland's
finest summit viewpoints. The ascent is demanding. The
path up the Allt Bealach Easain is our obvious approach, from
the col heading straight up for the top, a very steep 400 m.
Ben Tee is probably more often climbed from the east and,
with the next two hills, is very much part of the 'Loch Lochy
hills'.

Strong walkers could 'bag' the two Munros of Sron a'
Choire Ghairbh and Meall na Teanga but this is leaving little
time to cover the distance to Spean Bridge. Keep to the path
up to the Cam Bhealach (between the Munros) and ascend
them in turn from here. A useful stalkers' path heads up Sron
a' Choire Ghairbh. They are two fine, bold peaks, and show
well across Loch Lochy from the A82 road through the Great
Glen. They also look well from the group of hills west of our
day's pass and as these lie much more across the line of
travel they are another possibility for the day. They have the

added attraction of being little known, little visited hills so the description is given in greater detail. There are two Corbetts in the group.

Geal Charn—Meall na h-Eilde Hills

Immediately east of the bridge over the Greenfield Burn, below the house, is a small gate. Go through this and pick up a track which leads to a gate in the fence, beyond which the hillside is heathery and rapidly being covered in self-sown trees. The path is not easy to follow but keep parallel to and above the bank of the Greenfield Burn and it leads you to a gate in the forestry plantations. Go through this and follow the path up through the delicious shade of the woods. The going can be damp in places and the path is obviously no longer in regular use but its line is clear. One forestry road is crossed and, after a bigger stream, ensure you bear left. The path slowly comes back to follow the bank of the Greenfield Burn (heard if not seen) and then there is a gate out onto the moors from the corner of the wood. There are new plantings to the east but the area south is not affected.

Some gnarled old Scots pines by the river make a good resting spot. One tree has the lower stumps of branches polished by generations of stags rubbing their antlers on them. The path wanders up east of the burn to finish at a small 'meadow' in the hollow among the encircling hills. Thereafter one picks one's own route up the banks of the

The Commando Memorial —
a landmark for completing the
first stages of the walk.

stream, the Feadan nan Saobhaidh (the *chanter/flute* of *the fox den*) which starts in a peaty pool on the col between Meall Tarsuinn and Meall Coire nan Saobhaidh. Walk through the col, and turn up by a rising bank which is the end of another path which can clearly be seen descending off Meall Tarsuinn. Keep on rising steadily to flank round and up to the next col, between Meall Coire nan Saobhaidh and Geal Charn, the Bealach Carn na h-Urchaire, a pass of real character and grand views. Geal Charn beyond, is a Corbett, and its isolated position makes it an astonishing viewpoint to all the mountains of the west. A fence runs up to the summit trig point. The Cluanie Ridge looks satisfyingly distant and Ben Nevis dominates to the SE. A descent can be made southwards to Beinn Mheadhoin and Loch Arkaig or, from the Bealach Carn na h-Urchaire, the valley of the Allt Dubh followed down to Achnasaul. The once pleasant footpath has been bulldozed and gives rather unfriendly walking.

After an ascent of Geal Charn most mountaineers will turn east for Meall Coire nan Saobhaidh and Meall na h-Eilde. Corbett status, following the last mapping revisions, changed from the former peak to the latter. Meall na h-Eilde has good views to Meall na Teanga, the nearest Munro, and as one leaves its red summit rocks there is delightfully soft walking down green mossy grass slopes. Follow down to the Bealach an Easain (the col to Meall an t-Sagairt) before descending into Gleann Cia-aig, a descent which is brutally steep even by this easiest line. The main track through is joined just before the bridge over the Cia-aig and is followed as per the description on p 49.

From the summit of Geal Charn looking to the hills of Loch Arkaig and Knoydart.

Accommodation: Spean Bridge

Spean Bridge has a large number of guest houses, B&Bs, and a traditional hotel. The first to be met, just 200 metres before the commanding Commando Memorial is The Old Pines. Mrs Hamilton made us very welcome, despite our late arrival, and looked after us well. The view, like that from the Commando Memorial, is magnificent. Weary walkers, at the end of a long day, could hardly do better than stopping at The Old Pines. There are several other possibilities on the road down into Spean Bridge itself and every other house out the Glen Spean—Speyside A86 road offers accommodation. The hotel, like so many in the Highlands, is an old coaching inn and stands in the centre of the village. Behind it are one or two other B&Bs on the quiet road that runs along south of the River Spean.

Spean Bridge Hotel, Spean Bridge, PH24 4ES 0397 81 250

Spean Bridge Motor Inn, Spean Bridge, Inverness-shire 0397 81 351/366

Druimandarroch Guest House, Spean Bridge, PH34 4EU 0397 81 335

Curlevin (Mrs Duberley), Altour Road, Spean Bridge, Inverness-shire 0397 81 385

Inverour Guest House, Spean Bridge, Inverness-shire 0397 81 218

Grey Corrie's Guest House, Spean Bridge, Inverness-shire 0397 81 579

Coire Glas Guest House, Spean Bridge, PH34 4EU 0397 81 272

Barbagianni Guest House, Tirindrish, Spean Bridge, Inverness-shire 0397 81 437

Old Pines Guest House, Gairlochy Road, by Spean Bridge, Inverness-shire 0397 81 324

Camping Sites at Moy Farm 164828, Gairlochy (Mucomer) 188835, Stronaba 207845, but nothing in Spean Bridge itself; the surroundings are farming or forestry land so it is not too easy to find a quiet corner.

Shops There is a good store in Spean Bridge (no ECD) and between it and Telford's 1819 bridge is the Woollen Mill which has a cafe, open during the day. The RC chapel of St Joseph is an interesting modern building on the Corriechollie road. There is a Little Chef restaurant on the Fort William road.

Reading Broster, D. K.: *The Flight of the Heron*, 1925; *The Gleam in the North*, 1927; *The Dark Mile*, 1929. As one volume *A Jacobite Trilogy*, Penguin, 1984.
Cameron, A. D.: *The Caledonian Canal*, Dalton, 1972.
Rolt, L. C. T.: *Thomas Telford*, 1958.

Day 4

Forest tracks to Fort William and Glen Nevis

OS41

This is quite an easy day's walking — unless Ben Nevis is added to the programme — and the walk is described first without such diversions. In very hot conditions (not as uncommon as one might think) an early start pays dividends as the Leanachan Forest edge shades the track that is taken. Spean Bridge is left by the busy A82 road for Fort William: an unavoidable 1½ km of motor hazard which is escaped thankfully for the forest track.

Turn left onto the minor road, signposted Leanachan; the road right goes to Highbridge and Brackletter and Jacobite enthusiasts might like to walk along this road first for 1 km to see the ruins of High Bridge where the first shots of the Forty-Five were fired. At the news of the Prince's landing two companies of troops were sent from Fort Augustus to reinforce the Fort William garrison. They were observed and a party of twelve MacDonnells and a piper raced for the bridge and by appearing in different places, shouting various orders, shooting and piping convinced the government forces that the bridge was strongly held — causing them to retreat.

Immediately after going under the railway bridge on the Leanachan road turn right through a gate, the start of the 7 km forest edge road to Torlundy, easy walking with pleasant open views over the Great Glen. A stile near the end, to bypass a locked gate, is the most demanding effort on this stretch. Torlundy is a scattered hamlet with forestry offices, farm, etc. Turn right on the tarred road, over the railway, and so back to the A82 for the last 3 km to the outskirts of Fort William. The policies of the opulent Inverlochy Castle are on the west and the golf course lies to the east, backed by the heights of Ben Nevis. Those who don't mind carrying their packs high can now make for Ben Nevis from the Club House; described below.

A last bend brings one to the Distillery warehouses, left, and the busy junction of Victoria Bridge, the road heading west going to Glenfinnan and Mallaig. The filling station stocks a welcome selection of cold drinks and foodstuffs. Cut down to walk along the river bank (the now wide River Lochy), passing a sports complex, to reach Inverlochy Castle, the original, historic fortification. Not much remains but the strong corner towers and the 3-metre thick curtain walls give a lingering impression of strength. The National Gallery of Scotland has a Horatio McCulloch painting of the castle which shows it has not changed much in the last 150 years. This is not the fort that gave Fort William its name. That fort was built by Cromwell's man in Scotland, General Monck, in 1654, but fort and town names were apt to change. William is William of Orange so not surprisingly the Gaelic name translates as simply The Garrison. The fort was finally destroyed with the construction of the North British railway into the town but its gateway was moved to become the entrance to the local cemetery.

Alternative routes to Fort William

Before going on mention might be made of two other pleasant walks linking Spean Bridge with Fort William. Both are on sheet 41.

A. Instead of turning off the A82 left, into the Leanachan Forest, turn right onto a very quiet, minor surfaced road which makes a 10 km loop round by the Caledonian Canal to Torlundy. It passes High Bridge, noted above, them climbs up to give big views of the big Ben before running down the valley above the River Lochy.

B. Walk back to Gairlochy (morning views from the Commando Memorial) and follow the canal's south-side towpath down to Neptune's Staircase (a series of eight locks) at Banavie. The B8004 from Gairlochy to Banavie is not recommended as it has many blind corners and the views are the same from the safer canal banks. At 132792 the Torcastle approach road passes *under* the canal: an interesting feature built by Thomas Telford. The ruined Tor Castle was the former seat of Clan MacIntosh. Two other arches take the waters of the Allt Sheangain and all three arches are built with the curves of an inverted lock. The River Loy also flows under the canal, with big arches to cope with any spates. In the early years of the canal there were some near-disasters.

From Banavie it is possible to walk through Caol to a footbridge across the River Lochy to reach Inverlochy Castle — where the main route is joined again, or one could find accommodation in Banavie or Corpach.

From the castle take the footbridge across the aluminium smelter's water outflow and turn left to curve back onto the A82. Just beyond the entrance to the big works there is a bus stop on the west side of the road and a notice board indicating historical sites. Go up the small hill where there is an unexpectedly wide view from the indicator: a real mix of landscape and industry. Big pipes on the slopes of Ben Nevis are water pipes descending to the aluminium smelter. The waters are gathered from as far away as the headwaters of the River Spey and are fed through by Loch Laggan to Loch Treig and then by pipeline to Fort William to provide the electricity necessary for the smelting process. The Fort William museum has a good interpretive display on aluminium production, which contrasts a bit with its more historical aspects. Much of that history was fought out within sight of our small hilltop viewpoint. The (second) battle of Inverlochy in 1645 was part of an astonishing story of derring-do, concerning the Marquis of Montrose, who is one of the forgotten heroes of Scotland.

As our route from Spean Bridge to here is roughly the line taken by Montrose and Colkitto, looking down on the site of their victory is perhaps a good time for a brief history lesson. Rennie McOwan, a keen walker and historian, gave an account in an MBA Journal and with his permission I give most of it here. The events took place in the

The stark ruins of Inverlochy Castle near Fort William.

Walking up Glen Nevis on the north bank of the river. Sgurr a'Mhaim and the Stob Ban of the Mamores ahead.

bitter 17th century when religious bigotry and royal aggrandizement led to long years of bloody strife.

'James Graham, Marquis of Montrose, set out to win Scotland for Charles I and he was joined by Colkitto MacDonald, war leader of Clan Donald, who came from Ireland with an army of Irishmen, and who also wanted to restore the claims of Clan Donald to parts of Argyll, Kintyre and the West which had been lost to the expansionist policies of the Campbells who opposed Charles I.

'The MacDonalds had spread, harmoniously by marriage, to Antrim, hence the Irish connection. Colkitto is a corruption of the Gaelic, *ciotach*, meaning left-handed although it can also mean clever-cunning or ambidextrous.

'He is actually Alasdair McColla which in English would be Alexander, Son of Coll and, as he was later knighted by Charles I after the battle of Kilsyth, he is also known as Sir Alexander MacDonald or MacDonnell. But for the sake of brevity, he will be called Colkitto here.

'He was a superb soldier and there is a school of historical thought nowadays that it was he, and not Montrose, who was the brains behind their whirlwind campaign in 1645–46 which became known as the Year of Miracles.

'After some early tensions Colkitto and Montrose were joined by MacDonalds, Stewarts, Camerons, MacGregors and others. They thrashed a Covenant army at Tippermuir, outside Perth, and then captured and sacked Aberdeen. Then Colkitto suggested a winter march into the very heart of Argyll, to the Campbell capital of Inveraray, a blow at the most powerful of the Covenant families, and that is what they did. It caused a sensation and other clans and families joined Montrose and Colkitto. The Marquis of Argyll was taken off in a galley leaving his people to fend for themselves. The royalist army wintered there, burning and sacking Campbell lands.

'Then they pulled out and were back in the Great Glen, near present day Fort Augustus, when John Lom the bard of the Keppoch MacDonnells, brought the news that a Campbell army was only a few miles away, panting for revenge for the burning of Inveraray. From the north of the Great Glen came another hostile army under the Earl of Seaforth, and from the east yet another under the experienced General Baillie, one of the Scots mercenary generals so much in demand by European monarchs.

'Montrose and Colkitto decided to fight the strongest enemy first and they took to the hills in what has been described as a feat worthy of the Fianne, the mythical warriors of Gaeldom, and by John Buchan as one of the great feats of British arms. In the winter snows of 1645 they made their way over the hills to Inverlochy and there they had a crushing victory over the Campbells.

'For hill walkers, there has been much argument over the actual route of the 25-mile march, but there need not be. It is well documented if one knows where to look.

'Once one comes up the Corrieyairack pass above Culachy, the way is plain. A wooded side glen running parallel to the Great Glen is hidden from that glen by low hills (topped by a TV mast) and this leads through pleasant birches on to long flats, with great views to the hills further north and across the way to Ben Tee and its neighbours. By turning quickly off the line of the Corrieyairack the royalist army was concealed from below. These flats lead into Glen Buck and the army then made its way over an obvious plateau crossing to Glen Turret, and down that glen to the head of Glen Roy. At all times it was screened from the Great Glen.

'The army had an overnight stop in Glen Roy at Achavatee and then crossed the River Spean near Coirechoillie. They wended their way by the old townships of Kilchonate and Leanachan, now modern hill farms, to the slopes of Meall an t-Suidhe. They spent a second night out in freezing temperatures on snow-covered ground and with only enough food to feed part of the army and, in the morning, the sound of pipes told the astounded Campbells that their enemies were on them. Again the Marquis of Argyll left in a galley before the battle began.

'Montrose and Colkitto had other victories, at Auldearn in the north-west where Colkitto's bravery prevented the royalist army from being surprised and at Alford the only one of Montrose's victories at which Colkitto was not present as he was away recruiting in the west. They also won a crushing victory at Kilsyth, but King Charles' cause went down in England and Cromwell's star rose. The Catholicism of many of Colkitto's men was abhorrent to some Scots and many Lowland families held back. Montrose was surprised at Philiphaugh near Selkirk, when Colkitto was campaigning in the west, and defeated.

'Montrose went into exile, returned later and was defeated at Carbisdale in Sutherland, handed over to the Marquis of Argyll by MacLeod of Assynt and executed in Edinburgh. Colkitto fought on in the west and ravaged Argyll for a second time. Eventually he retreated to Ireland where he was to die in battle. Charles lost his head, most of Colkitto's Irishmen were killed, Clan Donald did not regain their ancient lands, and religious strife was to trouble Scotland and Ireland for many years.'

Follow the road almost into Fort William but just before the bridge across the River Nevis turn left (signposted for an industrial estate!) and follow up the north bank of the river. Fork right after some warehouses, etc and just before a *shop* on the corner. There is a footbridge (tubular-constructed) over the Nevis as this township of Claggan is left. There is a path of sorts all the way up by the River Nevis, sometimes by the river, sometimes by the field edge, sometimes cut by little side streams. A sturdy footbridge crosses from a big car park/picnic area on the west bank, a regular starting spot for ascending Ben Nevis. Cross here for the camp site. An improved path leads past Achintee House (see accommodation notes) where it turns up the hill and we turn right to continue along the wooded riverside for another kilometre to the youth hostel bridge, which is crossed to gain the hostel, forestry houses, shop and restaurant.

Ben Nevis

Ben Nevis, as Britain's highest summit, is a great lure to walkers of every sort — and to plenty of non-walkers too. In summer the Tourist Path is a Jacob's Ladder of people passing up and down. The ascent by the Tourist Path is relatively easy but the mountain is still a serious proposition because of its height, its chancy weather, and its cliffs and corries. It kills more people than the Eiger. Were it only slightly higher than its 1344 m there would be a permanent ice cap. As it is the average mean temperature is one degree below freezing. Snow can fall on the summit on any day of the year. 'And frequently does' the cynic may add. I've seen water in my cagoule pockets turn to ice on top but I've also strolled up in shorts and plimsolls. It all depends.

The experienced walker is capable enough to decide on his own doings but, for most, the Tourist Path is the best way up. The old pony path starts at Achintee, which is also reached by a bridge from the car park on the west bank of the River Nevis. The path rises steadily across the flank of Meall an t-Suidhe (Mel-an-tee). Another path comes up from the youth hostel bridge and has required restoration work to deal with erosion. After some zig-zags the path bears round into the Red Burn hollow and the col holding Lochan Meall an t-Suidhe.

On the path rising up and across to the Red Burn again stood what was known as the Half Way Hut. The next 300 m is a continuous zig-zag up bouldery slopes before the angle eases for the summit plateau, 'the Plateau of Storms'. The great northern cliffs bite into the plateau and on the south boulder slopes lead down to big corries and gullies. There is no room for casual navigation and in bad conditions, and in winter conditions, the novice walker should leave well alone: better a living rabbit than a dead hero.

Heroes there have been in plenty and Ken Crocket's history of the hill makes compulsive reading. The first Saturday in September sees the Ben Nevis Race. The record for this run up and down the mountain from Fort William is about 1 hour 25 minutes. Early August each year sees a race on airbeds down the River Nevis — and that takes in the Lower Falls! Heroic too, perhaps, are the hundreds each year who have never climbed any hill till they set off to climb the Ben. Long live the fun of adventure, at whatever level.

Being the highest hill the summit view is extensive but not beautiful. One could as well be in a balloon. Ireland can be seen 120 miles to the south, the hills north of Inverness can

The great cliffs of Ben Nevis (in May).

be named and from Cairngorms to Outer Hebrides the eye can follow the sweep of the day. Sunrise or sunset are times to be on top of Scotland. It then feels the top of the world.

In summer other routes besides the Tourist Track can be considered. The Allt a' Mhuilinn (*stream of the mill*) which drains the huge *cirque* north of the Ben has a path well

The view south from the summit of Ben Nevis.

tramped out alongside it. One path starts at the golf course clubhouse, crosses the golf course and heads up by the burn, another starts at the distillery opposite Victoria Bridge and follows the river across to the steeper slopes where path or maintenance roads lead one upward. One variation swings up by the Allt Coire an Lochain to Lochan Meall an t-Suidhe and this is the approach used by the Model T Ford in 1911 and other stunt ascents since. A path also heads north above this loch to circle round and up the Allt a' Mhuilinn. Set under the cliffs is the SMC (Scottish Mountaineering Club) hut, 'the CIC' (Charles Inglis Clark memorial hut). The path ends in Coire Leis and, clear of snow, it is possible to scramble up the headwall onto the col between Ben Nevis and Carn Mor Dearg. The knife-edge ridge linking them is the famous Carn Mor Dearg Arête, a foreign name now hallowed by tradition. Steep boulder slopes lead from the Arête to the top of the Ben and the descent of this route is extremely dangerous in mist due to the slope peeling over onto the cliffs. Several fatalities have occurred with climbers slipping on snow and plunging down into Coire Leis. For the strong walker a circuit over the Ben, the Arête and Carn Mor Dearg is a superb expedition. The French have a saying that experience is the sum of near misses. Don't miss out on the Ben!

If Ben Nevis is a prime objective on the crossing one pleasant alternative is to walk down from Spean Bridge to Torlundy (described already) then, instead of continuing to Fort William or Glen Nevis, book into accommodation, and set off for Ben Nevis from Torlundy. The golf course route starts just 1 km down the A82. Kinlochleven can be reached the following day as planned.

Accommodation: Torlundy

The Factor's House, Torlundy, Fort William, Inverness-shire, PH33 6SN. 0397 5767

Mrs Campbell, Lea Sona, Torlundy, Fort William, Inverness-shire. 0397 4661

Mrs Matheson, Thistle Cottage, Torlundy, Fort William, Inverness-shire. 0397 2428

Mrs Cameron, Aonach Mor, The Bungalow, Torlundy, Fort William, Inverness-shire. 0397 4525

Aonach Mor is the last of the line of forestry houses east of the A82 (148771), the other B&Bs are west of the A82 (142771, 141773) while The Factor's House is just off the A82, also on the west. This is a somewhat up-market hotel and an evening meal could cost more than a B&B — but the food is good and a deserved reward for climbing Ben Nevis. Inverlochy Castle, further on, is a huge, luxurious mansion which is probably beyond the financial resources of most walkers! Queen Victoria stayed a week at Inverlochy before sailing along the Caledonian Canal on one of her wanderings from Balmoral.

Spean Bridge to Kinlochleven
OS41

This is a long day's tramp, following old drovers' routes, so it does not go up onto the summits, but still takes in some impressive scenery. For those who do not want to visit Fort William or the Nevis or Mamore hills this route gives a memorable alternative. If other hills are wanted there are bothies at the Lairig Leacach 283736 and Meanach 264684 but sleeping bags and camping gear would have to be carried.

Turn up towards the station in Spean Bridge, then fork left, passing the modernistic Catholic church and continue eastwards over the railway and along riverside woodlands. Follow the tarred road up to Corriechoille and then turn southwards towards the hills by the line of a very historic drovers' route, which reaches 510 m at the top of the pass, a deep gap between the Grey Corries and the Innse Corbetts. Lairig Leacach means _pass of the flagstones_. The bothy is at the end of the estate road and, just beyond, turn right to follow the Penny Pass over and down to Luibeilt. The Abhainn Rath has to be forded and Luibeilt is now a ruin. An estate road runs from there to Kinlochleven via Mamore Lodge or you can cut down directly to the village by a more direct footpath.

This is only a brief summary of the route and those seeking the hills _en route_ should be capable of their own planning.

The hills are big, often covered in screes high up and far from any civilization, which is both an attraction and a warning. The useful height already gained by being on this route makes the Munros and Corbetts available especially attractive.

Accommodation: Glen Nevis/ Fort William

Fort William gives the impression of being all hotels and B&Bs, but many are expensive or out of the town on the Glen Coe side so not really convenient for Glen Nevis or the Ben. Listed below are some on the north side of the town and in Glen Nevis itself. Failing these consult the Fort William Tourist Centre, Cameron Square, Fort William, 0397 3781, or obtain their accommodation list in advance. They list over seventy B&Bs and 37 hotels and guest houses!

Nevis Bank Hotel   0397 2595
   (At the road junction at the entrance to Glen Nevis, next to big restaurant.)
Milton Hotel, North Road, Fort William, Inverness-shire. 0397 2331
Ben View Guest House, Belford Road, Fort William. 0397 2966   (Between viewpoint and roundabout).
Craig Nevis West Guest House, Belford Road, Fort William, PH33 6BU.   0397 2023
Glenlochy Guest House, Nevis Bridge, Fort William, Inverness-shire.   0397 2909

In Glen Nevis
B&Bs Mrs Thompson, Tignabruaich, Glen Nevis, Fort William, Inverness-shire.   0397 2182 (122732)
   Mrs Macdonald, 7 Glen Nevis, Fort William, Inverness-shire.
   0397 4688   (One of the forestry houses).

Achintee: A complex of historical buildings which have been modernized to offer Farm Guest House, self-catering cottage, apartments and bunkhouse accommodation.

Achintee, Fort William, Inverness-shire.
0397 2240/3667

Glen Nevis Youth Hostel (127716), Fort William, Inverness-shire, PH33 6ST. 0397 2336.
A grade I hostel with 128 beds but its proximity to Ben Nevis and the termination of the West Highland Way makes it popular and it is·often full. Booking is advisable, and essential at holiday weekends and in July and August. Store in hostel.

Camping Only on the sites. There is a very small site just 100 m up the Glen Nevis road from the A82 roundabout, and a very big, well-appointed, site $2\frac{1}{2}$ km up the glen, almost next door to the restaurant and 500 m from the youth hostel: Glen Nevis Camping and Caravan Park, by Fort William, Inverness-shire, PH33 6SX. 0397 2191

Glen Nevis Restaurant and Bar, 0397 5459, serves meals from noon onwards and is recommended (7-day licence).

Nevisport High Street, Fort William, Inverness-shire. 0397 4921 Has a good restaurant and coffee bar and, as well as mountaineering gear, has a wide selection of books on mountains, wildlife, Scottish and local interest.

Swimming pool Belford Road, is on the Nevis side of town. Open 10.00 am–8.00 pm summer weekdays, 12.30–4.00 pm weekends.

West Highland Museum is in Cameron Square, near the Tourist Centre, and has interesting exhibits, well presented, on local history, Jacobite history, geology, coins, archaeology, maps and weapons. Open office hours, but in summer from 9.30 am to 9.00 pm.

Reading Buchan, J.: *Montrose*, 1928 (readable account).
Crocket, K. V.: *Ben Nevis*, Scottish Mountaineering Club, 1986 (excellent history).
Kilgour, W. T.: *Twenty Years on Ben Nevis*, Ernest Press, 1985 (Observatory life).
MacOwan, R.: *Ben Nevis*, Lang Syne, 1986 (booklet, stories).

Murray, W. H.: *Mountaineering in Scotland*, Dent, 1947, *Undiscovered Scotland*, Dent, 1951. (Both in one volume, Diadem, 1979.)

Royal Meteorological Society: *Ben Nevis Observatory 1883–1904* (Centenary booklet, available from Nevisport).

Tranter, N.: *Montrose* (1-volume edition of historical novels *The Young Montrose* and *Montrose, the Captain General*).

Ben Nevis–Mamores

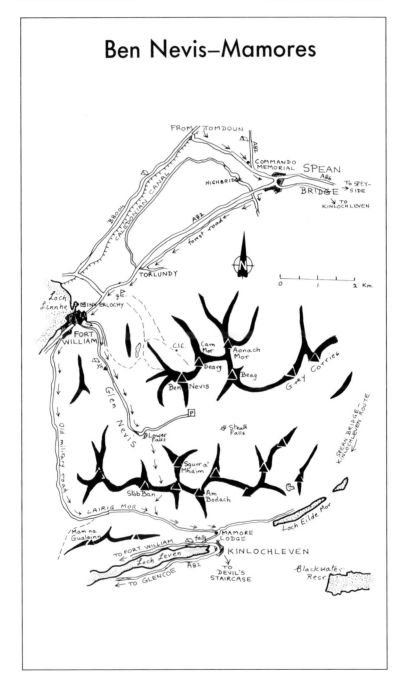

Day 5

Passes or peaks to Kinlochleven

OS41

A range of big hills, the Mamores, bars the route to Kinlochleven and has to be either climbed or circumambulated. There is also a compromise as the easy route of the West Highland Way comes over the western rump of the Mamores into Glen Nevis rather than just following the road into Fort William. Based as we are in Glen Nevis this is the logical route if not wanting a high hill crossing over the Mamores, and is described first.

A. The Lairigmor

The *great* or *big pass* is part of the 1749–50 military road built by Wade's successor Toby Caulfeild. It is a good, if rough track, between Blar a' Chaorainn and Kinlochleven while, from Blar a' Chaorainn into Fort William, it is a tarred road. The West Highland Way cuts off from Blar a' Chaorainn (*plain of the rowans*) to cut over into Glen Nevis.

The start for the road is at the big roundabout at the south end of Fort William, signposted Upper Achintore, a road which pulls up with brutal steepness — one way of gaining instant views, of Loch Linnhe and the west and of Ben Nevis peering over the near slopes. 'Peat road', left, is a track leading through to Glen Nevis and indicates where at one time the villages cut peat for fuel. The road rather switchbacks for the next stretch. Blarmachfoldach is an old hamlet which had a certain fame from refusing to observe

British Summer Time, holding to 'God's time' instead. As late as 1950 they also observed the Old New Year of 12 January — the rest of the country having changed in 1752.

At Blar a' Chaorainn there is a view to pretty Lochan Lunn Da Bhra with its few Scots pines. A good walk heads through to the Corran narrows. A water bull (*tarbhuisge*) lived in the loch according to local folklore. Before continuing with the Lairigmor we must describe the West Highland Way route from Glen Nevis to Blar a' Chaorainn.

There are two starting points in Glen Nevis, both clearly signposted. One route starts just south of the Clan Cameron

Left *The Lower Falls, Glen Nevis.*

Below *From the Tourist Path up Ben Nevis looking across to the Mamores: Sgurr a'Mhaim (left) and Stob Ban (centre) — the suggested crossing uses the col between them.*

cemetery/car park area (123727) and follows the peat road up into the forest, then turns left (south) along a forestry road. (The peat road can also be followed straight over the hills; it joins a good dirt road down to the Lundarva road just above the last houses of Fort William.) The other begins beside the restaurant and takes the road up past the forestry houses into the trees and, when it meets the traversing forestry road, turns right (north). After about 4–500 m walking along either route one comes on a junction and the West Highland Way is indicated following the uphill road. This rises gradually southwards for $1\frac{1}{2}$ km at which point the route abandons the forest road to zig-zag uphill through the trees. This change is clearly indicated of course. The path up has already caused erosion needing remedial work, our modern Way being far less skilfully created than the old stalkers' paths.

The path crosses a col on the crest of the hills and the bump on the left is worth a detour being the site of a vitrified hill fort named Dun Deardail. Vitrification was caused by the deliberate(?) fusion by fire of timber-laced stone ramparts. Such forts are found from the Argyll coast right through to Easter Ross and are attributed to Celtic colonizers. Many have the feel of being strategically placed watch towers. Dun Deardail is now largely overgrown.

The Way makes a 5 km sweep round to the Lairigmor, passing through trees for much of the distance and running alongside the old head-dyke of the glen's cultivation. Statistics of 1812 showed 150–200 people once lived hereabouts. The underlying rock is a richer limestone, which offered better pasture. Now only a few crofts remain, at Blarmachfoldach, the rest is Sitka spruce (whose introduction lies at the door of the Scone lad David Douglas, whose name is however given to a more welcome fir). At the derelict cottage of Blar a' Chaorainn we join the old military road from Fort William.

The plantations continue for another 2 km. A sheepfold lies beside the edge of the trees, the last touch of civilization as the singularly empty, bleak glen, curves ahead, impressive in a barren way but hardly beautiful. In either lashing storms or beating sun it must have been very unpopular with the poor redcoats. The glen is devoid of shelter. Place names are ruined or derelict houses. I've seen us cringe below bridges to escape storms and I've seen us jump into burns fully clothed to counteract the roasting glare of summer heatwave conditions.

At Lairigmor a right-of-way cuts over the shoulder of Mam na Gualainn (a Corbett with a mighty view) to Callert on Loch Leven. A ferry at one time operated across to Glen Coe and the route was also a coffin road with the dead being taken out to Eilean Munde (*the isle of the world*). Islands were popular burial spots, as wolves could not dig up the bodies. As a boy I was rowed to the island by a local and was indiscreet enough to mention the name Campbell. The old man stopped rowing and deliberately spat into the sea. At one time there was reputedly a pub in Glen Coe which had a notice saying 'No dogs. No Campbells'. Later a more tolerant owner changed the sign, removing the prohibition on dogs.

Tigh-na-sleubhaich, just before the watershed, was a reasonable building until the West Highland Way opened, now it is ruinous. The road still manages to put in some uphill stretches as it slowly wends out of the claustrophobic pass. The rich landscape of the head of Loch Leven appears. You may even hear the echoing blast of a factory hooter as the day's work ends at the aluminium smelting works that look so strange down in Kinlochleven. At a spur (Mam-Mor, *big pass*, on old maps) the West Highland Way deserts the high-level road to drop to sea-level. The road keeps on round to Mamore Lodge, passing a TV booster station on the way and a sign at the parting of the ways holds out the temptations of the lodge to weary walkers: drinks and food, baths and beds. Why drop 300 m to Kinlochleven just to climb it all again on the morrow? Another choice to be made!

The route down is obvious enough, running through attractive forest, crossing the Mamore Lodge drive and debouching beside a garage near the school on the outskirts of Kinlochleven.

B. Over the Mamores
OS41

There is one mountaineers' alternative to the West Highland Way which is well worth the effort *in good conditions*: the pass over the Mamores between Stob Ban and Sgurr an Iubhair (the 1001 m but nameless summit on the map). The ascent has a strangely alpine feel and the long view down Glen Nevis is unusual and quite spectacular. Several Munros can be added to the crossing.

Wherever one is staying cross over the bridge at the youth hostel (at the latest) to walk up the east bank of the River Nevis. There is now a path all the way and the walking is far more pleasant than on the tarred road with its traffic. Pass east of the Old Grave Yard, marked by big beeches and sycamores and note just beforehand, a solitary multiple beech. I suspect, when the graveyard was planted, there were young beeches left over and they were just planted together — and survived, their many trunks making a single tree.

At the last bend make a rising contour up the hillside to Polldubh. Two cottages are passed and a farm track leads from them to the sheep fank by the glen road at the Lower Falls. The road switches from south to north side of the River Nevis here and more or less crosses a gorge with split cascades — an interesting spectator point for the annual Raft Race! The crags on the Ben Nevis side are the Polldubh Crags, a popular low-level rock-climbing area. If you keep eyes, and ears, open you may observe the ballerinas in action.

Cross the second stile once over the bridge and follow up the Allt Coire a' Mhusgain path. This is an old stalkers' path and makes for easy going. After a crag is passed the path turns straight up the hill in a series of loops before traversing along at a higher level. Take care not to go charging on and miss this turning. Stob Ban appears as a ragged, rocky peak of peaks and both its character, the feel of exposure as one wends above the corrie, and the view right down Glen Nevis, give this the alpine flavour on which so many comment. When the path crosses the burn at the top hollow (the path can be seen zig-zagging up to the col) it is as easy to head straight up to the charming, spring-fed lochan held under the slabby cliffs of Sgurr an Iubhair. This is a delectable spot for a picnic but do please leave no litter. (Last time there we had to wade icy waters to remove beer cans from the lochan.)

Stob Ban, Sgurr an Iubhair, Sgurr a' Mhaim and Am

Bodach are all Munros, so it is tempting to climb some or all of them. Stob Ban is a *white peak* of shattered quartz rocks. A path contours from the lochan to the col then up a grassy shoulder before the final rocky summit slopes. A gully bites in just below the summit so care needs to be taken, particularly on descent, if there is mist. Mullach nan Coirean to the west is a contrastingly red hill (granite). Return to the col and, if no other peaks are climbed, there is the option of using the path shown that heads south west down and round below Stob Ban, leaving it at its lowest point to make a knee-battering, steep descent to the Lairigmor road (West Highland Way/Old Military Road).

A better descent can be made with little extra exertion by taking in Sgurr an Iubhair as well. From the lochan a fine series of zig-zags (Jacob's Ladder we've always called it) takes one up to the col due north of Sgurr an Iubhair. This is only one of many paths the OS do not show on the map for the Mamore Forest. (Forest is more or less synonymous with mountain range, referring to deer forest and not a forest with trees.) Paths wend up to Sgurr an Iubhair from this col, which gives a sudden, bold view to the central Mamore peaks and by heading south the skirting path is reached. Use it down to the Am Bodach col (Am Bodach another tempting Munro) then, after a brutal descent southwards from the saddle, the stalkers' path down Coire na h-Eirghe is utilized down to the Lairigmor.

Sgurr a' Mhaim, which so dominates the view up Glen Nevis, and whose quartz topping is often taken for snow, is also a possibility from the top of Jacob's Ladder but the ridge to the peak is not called the Devil's Ridge without reason: an up-and-down crest with several bits of scrambling, some exposure and needing some experience in the walker tackling it. There is a clear path all the way however. Done as part of this day the traverse has to be reversed so, if time is short or

Top left *Reaching the Mamores crest — approaching the col with Stob Ban, the peak in the background.*

Above left *In the Lairig Mor, the great pass (old military road) from Fort William to Kinlochleven.*

Left *Approaching the eyrie–like Mamore Lodge from the Lairig Mor track.*

the ridge still has snow on it, the Devil's Ridge is best left for another visit.

From the col between Stob Ban and Sgurr an Iubhair the descent to the Lairigmor is very steep, but the path shown can make this less arduous though it has an annoying re-ascent before cutting across the craggier SW spur of Stob Ban to reach the easy slopes of the corrie above Tigh-na-Sleubhaich (*the house by the gullied slopes*). The temptation to cut down direct from the lowest point of the path should be resisted. If a short-cut is taken the best line is to ignore the path altogether and descend by the burn from the col. The path is best — its builders knew what they were doing.

The eyrie-like perch of Mamore Lodge, as mentioned before, is an alternative to Kinlochleven for overnight accommodation. People drive up from the town for bar suppers and an atmosphere that is something different. The setting is magnificent and in May the scent of the yellow azaleas wafts in the windows. Mamore Lodge was built by the aluminium company as part of a deal when they took over the estate's original lodge by the River Leven — an industrial complex was not exactly welcomed by the gentry, in this case the Bibby family of shipping fame. In 1935 however the company bought up the whole Mamore estate. King Edward VII, a great slaughterer of deer and grouse (and one of the great marksmen of his era) stayed at the lodge in 1909 when he shot nine stags. On my last crossing two of our party stayed in what had been the royal suite (the third member camped — a decision only enjoyed by the midges). Without in any way detracting from Kinlochleven I'd recommend staying at the lodge, even if planning to cross the Devil's Staircase the next day. Not many walkers on the Way care to come up at the day's end, which is to our advantage. It is also possible to stay high on a route which avoids any descent to sea-level.

Kinlochleven is an unpretentious industrial village which has somehow strayed into a superb Highland setting. It owes its existence to the setting up of an aluminium smelting works in 1904 and this remains the town's *raison d'être*. Being deeply set at the head of a sea *fjord* the village counteracts the winter weeks without any sun by painting its houses in varied colours. Compared to Ballachulish and Onich, at either end of the bridge that left Kinlochleven such a backwater, the atmosphere is down-to-earth working class. There is even a chip shop! There are quite a few shops and, being on the pedestrian main road of the West Highland Way, there are plenty of B&B facilities. There is a certain irony that, after days of hard walking, we are technically still on the western seaboard.

Kinlochleven is something of an artificial name; north of the river was originally Kinlochmore, and south of the river was Kinlochbeg. These were just tiny settlements and shooting lodges before the works were created prior to World War 1. The Mamore Estate resisted expansion north of the river till bought out in 1935 and when houses were built there were some ridiculous results as the River Leven was the boundary between Argyll and Inverness-shire. For instance, there were two police stations, one on each side of the river (in a town hardly needing one station), and criminals were taken off to Oban or Fort William depending on which side of the river an offence occurred. Most of these absurdities went in the 1975 reorganization but that year also saw the Balluchulish Bridge opened and Kinlochleven reverted to being a bit of a backwater. Postally or with dialling codes both sides are still called Kinlochleven, even if the post office is in Kinlochbeg. The OS add to confusion by using the names Kinlochmore and Kinlochleven on the map.

I can recall studying ferry queues at Ballachulish. If there were more than a certain number of cars we'd drive round Loch Leven rather than wait. The road from Glen Coe to Kinlochleven was only built during the First World War,

Loch Leven and the sweeping bulk of Garbh Bheinn which dominates Kinlochleven.

The odd spectacle of heavy industry in the wilds — the aluminium works at Kinlochleven.

largely by PoW labour. Before then the normal approach to the town was by sea, the shores having the roughest of tracks.

Extra days at Kinlochleven

You could spend a week very easily at Kinlochleven if interested in Munros and/or Corbetts. Loch Leven is pinched between two Corbetts, another lies to the east while the Mamores offer a seemingly endless number of Munros. The more westerly Mamore Munros have been mentioned already. On our heatwave 1988 coast-to-coast walk we took a day extra at Mamore Lodge to 'bag' more Mamores — and were promptly snowed on. But by then we had wandered up Coire na Ba to Na Gruagaichean and were lunching on An Garbhanach. Stob Coire a' Chairn and Am Bodach were then traversed in a rattle of snow but it cleared for the descent under Stob Coire na h-Eirghe back to the Lairig Mor track. At lower levels there had been less pleasant rain. On Na Gruagaichean we had almost been lured to turning east for graceful Binnean Mor but the best round of that Mamore extremity is to use the path up to Coire an Lochain, sclim Sgurr Eilde Mor, use the path again to add Binnein Beag and return over Binnein Mor to Na Gruagaichean, descending by the south ridge. Two great circuits. The Mamores offer some of the best high-level traversing in Britain and, if well tracked, there are still parts where a head for heights and the use of hands will be necessary. They are big, rough hills quite capable of dirty tricks.

Garbh Bheinn is the masculine hill that keeps the sun off Kinlochleven for months at a time. It can be climbed (or traversed) by the ridge facing the town. North of Loch Leven a path from 237 on the Lairig Mor track tempts one onto the Beinn na Caillich—Mam na Gualainn traverse, the latter another Corbett with a mighty view. Glas Bheinn between the Loch Eildes and the Blackwater is also a Corbett, rather unexciting in itself but with good views.

If not planning summits then a visit to the astonishing Grey Mare's Waterfall followed by the high traverse round to the Blackwater dam, with a return down the River Leven glen, is a must — as fine a walk as you will find in Scotland.

Kinlochleven may not be Kleine Scheidegg but it is 'mighty fine' as an American partner declared.

Accommodation: Kinlochleven

Mamore Holiday Lodge, Kinlochleven, Argyll, PA40 4QN. 08554 213

Mrs Robertson, 4 Loch Eilde Road, Kinlochleven, Argyll. 08554 358

Mrs Young, 6 Lochaber Crescent, Kinlochleven, Argyll. 08554 332

Mrs Young, 6 Mamore Road, Kinlochleven, Argyll. 08554 215

Mrs Budge, 'Greymares', Wades Road, Kinlochleven, Argyll. 08554 334

Mrs Napier, 'Tigh-na-Cheo', Garbhein Road, Kinlochleven, Argyll. (DB&B) 08554 434

Mrs MacNeil, 24 Wades Road, Kinlochleven, Argyll. 08554 459

Narrach Bridge Caravan Site (for B&B), Kinlochleven, Argyll. 08554 266

Miss MacAngus, 'Hermon', Kinlochleven, Argyll. 08554 383

Mrs Walsh, 'Ard na Seileach', Kinlochleven, Argyll. 08554 323

Mrs Downes, 'Mardon', Kinlochleven, Argyll. 08554 609

Mrs Watt, 14 Wades Road, Kinlochleven, Argyll.

Mrs MacKenzie, 'Innistone', Wades Road, Kinlochleven, Argyll. 08554 260

Mrs MacDonald, 19 Mamore Road, Kinlochleven, Argyll. 08554 259

Mrs Long, 12 Lochaber Road, Kinlochleven, Argyll. 08554 323

Camping Narrach Bridge Caravan Site (08554 266) is pleasant — on the north side of the loch 2 km west from Kinlochleven.

Shops There are all the village shops one would expect. No early closing day. Laundrette. Harlequin Restaurant and Bakery is open seven days a week (also carry-outs).

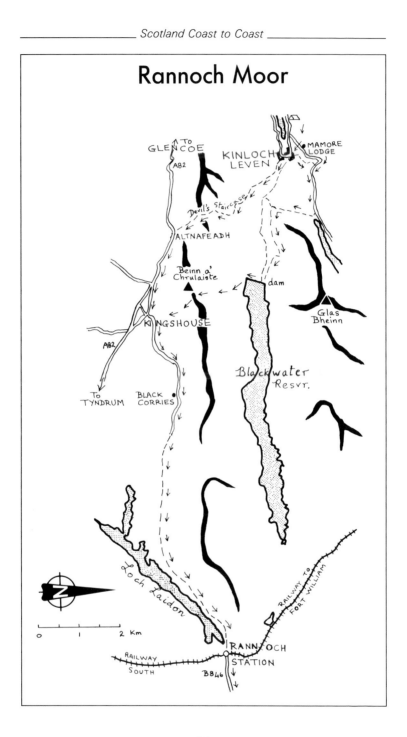

Rannoch Moor

Day 6

Onto Rannoch Moor

OS41

One is more or less forced to go to the Kingshouse as there is no accommodation elsewhere. Strong walkers could go Kinlochleven — Rannoch Station in one day but this should be a planned rather than a snap decision. The crossing of the Moor is a serious undertaking. There are several routes to choose from to reach the Kingshouse from Kinlochleven. The beaten track (*very* beaten seeing it is part of the West Highland Way) is over the old military road, the Devil's Staircase. An alternative is to walk up the spectacular River Leven to the Blackwater dam and take the pass SW between Beinn Beag and Beinn a' Chrulaiste or the pass southwards between Beinn a' Chrulaiste and Meall Bhalach. If starting from Mamore Lodge keep on the high track round to Loch Eilde Mor and then follow the pipeline from it to the Blackwater, via the Leitir Bo Fionn. This is sufficiently spectacular that (on a clear day) I'd recommend it even for folk starting at sea-level. Take one of the paths up to the high road (visiting the Grey Mare's Waterfall on the way) and the next few miles offer quite unrivalled scenery. It reminds me of Norway. In 1988 three of us (one was 68) went from Mamore Lodge to Blackwater to the col, climbed Chrulaiste, cut round to the Black Corries road and on to Rannoch Station. The weather was perfect but it was still a thirteen-hour day — an unforgettable one.

The surroundings of Kinlochleven are a maze of horizontal and vertical paths, all deeply set in a birch forest jungle, full of crags and waterfalls and ruins. (Real Bevis country, a marvellous place to explore as a child.) For brevity and clarity I've only mentioned some of the possible routes and all have been described from a start in the middle of Kinlochmore, north of the bridge over the River Leven. The people must be very religious (or the opposite?) for there are four churches: Church of Scotland (a trim, white and grey building), a small Catholic chapel, the United Free Church (a wooden hut) and the Episcopal Church of St Paul's, where the good ladies provide teas in the hall.

A. By the Devil's Staircase

Just north of the bridge over the River Leven there is a notice board indicating the West Highland Way. The path drops down to join the river bank path (which comes out from under the road bridge) and wends upstream, with a tarred surface, to reach a housing scheme in a very rural setting. The tail race from the aluminium works explodes into the river rather dramatically.

Turn right at the road and walk along the neat, garden-conscious row of houses. The road bends left and becomes a footpath which is followed to a bridge across the River Leven. Below it are some deep, black pools and, just above, a band of red rock runs through the grey quartzite. It can also be seen on the bank as one curls up onto a spur where there is a sudden view of the aluminium works. A works road is joined and a bridge leads across the six black pipes of the works power station. There are several notices there to catch the descending West Highland Waywardmen. Turn left and follow the works road up beside the pipeline to the first spur. A right fork is taken, to wend up Coire Mhorair and zig-zag to the next spur and the top buildings of the pipeline (300 m), which is much steeper in this upper section.

The road continues on up the valley, roughly on the line of the aqueduct bringing the water from the Blackwater Reservoir (see p 94). Across the valley the horizontal line is a later aqueduct tapping the waters of Loch Eilde Mor and taking them to the Blackwater (more PoW labour). We tend to forget just how early this power scheme was. Hydro-electric schemes only really peaked after World War 2.

The riverbank path (part of the West Highland Way) in Kinlochleven — start of the approach of the Devil's Staircase.

The West Highland Way breaks off (clearly signposted) for its continuing ascent. There are good views back. The path crosses the two Choire Odhair streams and the spur between, the setting becoming progressively wilder and bleak, before a last pull up to the cairn marking the top of the Devil's Staircase, a rather bleak and featureless spot. The cairn will no doubt prove a welcome resting spot, and a chance for a last look at the breaking-wave ranges of the Mamore peaks with Ben Nevis looming beyond. To the south stand the two Buachailles and Bidean in Glen Coe, highest summit in Argyll. Beyond the Buachaille Etive Mor lies Rannoch Moor. There is a great 'feel' to crossing this pass, only bettered perhaps by the alternative that takes in Beinn a' Chrulaiste. When we drop down onto the Moor we are on the high heart of Scotland and not till we leave the hills at the end will we lose the height gained today.

The Massacre of Glen Coe has a place of notoriety in our history but the number killed might have been higher had the road over the Devil's Staircase existed at that date (1692). One contingent of soldiers was to cross the pass and cut off any escape from the top of the glen but they ran into a blizzard and did not win over till after the event. The story is well told in the books by John Buchan or John Prebble (and both are in paperback at present), so I'll just give a brief summary of a complex affair, which was all too typical of its period rather than the horrifying event it is usually painted. There is a connection too with the Battle of Killiecrankie in 1689, the site of which we see later on.

Glencoe men took part in the battle and, in typical fashion, made the most of their time away from home, raiding through Glen Lyon on the way home and returning with a booty of goods and beasts. In 1691 the clans were told to take an oath of allegiance to King William before the end of the year, or face reprisals. MacIan of Glencoe (Glencoe is the village, Glen Coe is the glen), for various reasons, only set off on the last day of the year to present himself at Fort William, only to find that he should have gone to Inveraray. The Governor of the Fort packed him off with a letter to Campbell of Ardkinglas, the Sheriff Depute. Severe weather intervened. MacIan arrived on the 2nd but Ardkinglas was away until the 5th and only administered the oath on the 6th but warned the lateness would have to be reported. MacIan set off home believing all was well.

But the government authorities comprising both English and Scots were already embarked on devious repressive schemes and Secretary of State Dalrymple decided to make an example of the Glencoe MacDonalds on the flimsy excuse that they had not submitted in time. (Several other clans were in the same position and nothing was done about them.) William was embroiled in war with France and gave his approval to 'extirpate that sept of thieves'. On 1 February 1692 some 120 soldiers of Argyll's Regiment, commanded by Campbell of Glen Lyon, were quartered on the people of Glen Coe. Campbell of Glenlyon was actually related by marriage to MacIan and even though his lands had been raided he was taken in with accustomed hospitality.

On the 12th orders went out for the massacre and 400 men set off by the Devil's Staircase route to close the upper glen but blizzards held them up so they did not arrive till mid-morning on the 13th. By then, it was all over. At 5.00 am MacIan was roused from bed and shot in the back, his wife so dreadfully misused that she died and the massacre commenced, all under seventy being put to the sword. About forty were killed but many escaped into the storm (some to die of exposure) and one suspects that the ordinary troops were not too keen on carrying out their orders. A story was told by one soldier many years later, when once again under a roof in Glen Coe, how he had only cut off a finger from a child he'd been ordered to kill. The host silently held up a hand with one finger missing.

The massacre caused a public outcry and eventually a commission of inquiry was set up in 1695. Dalrymple lost his Secretaryship (and was given a pension!), but nobody was seriously inconvenienced by a good whitewash job. The memory remains, a bitter taste of a singularly nasty episode.

Below us, in the mouth of the pass between the two Buachailles is Lochan na Fola (*the lochan of blood*) which commemorates a 1543 rustling party being wiped out by the pursuing owners of the lifted cattle, so the famous massacre was only one episode of a long story of bloodshed.

The Lairig Gartain is a textbook glaciated valley but it is also part of a geological fault running (as many do) from SW to NE. I first became aware of it when walking down the Allt an Inbhir from Loch Chiarain to the Blackwater. I was in a tight, straight wee glen and across the reservoir the pass between Chrulaiste and Beinn Bheag was in line and, beyond again, the Lairig Gartain: V inside V inside V, it was like looking along a gun barrel.

This descent route is the Devil's Staircase proper (the name now tends to be given to the whole pass) and this name, or nickname, probably originated among the hundreds of officers and men of Rich's and Guise's Regiments who were involved in the road's construction. The date was 1750, long after General Wade (the great roadbuilder) had left Scotland. This is a Caulfeild road, as are others so often credited to Wade. Roy's map of that period gave the pass the name Mam Grianan (*the pass of the sheltered nook* or *bower*) which only goes to show sarcasm is nothing new. The pass is singularly exposed and featureless and in misty conditions the track should be followed carefully. The hairpins are still clear despite the erosion of two centuries but however good the road originally one can but admire travellers of the period who crossed the Devil's Staircase by coach. The route comes down to the main road 50 m west of Altnafeadh, a shepherd's house standing among some trees. The white building across under the Buachaille is Lagangarbh, the Scottish Mountaineering Club's hut. Beware of speeding motorists on this bit of the A82.

Keep to the West Highland Way, which quickly leaves the A82 east of Altnafeadh and, with a bit of hopscotch with fences, follows the old Military Road, wandering along the hillside before turning down to join the minor road that leads to the Kingshouse Hotel. The ruin passed is of the Queenshouse, a companion inn, which has long disappeared. As we turn right, following the road to the hotel, a rougher estate road (signposted 'Rannoch by Loch Laidon') heads on into the Moor — our route for tomorrow. A fine old bridge over the adolescent River Etive lands us at the door of the Kingshouse.

B. River Leven and the Blackwater

Start off as for the West Highland Way but, once past the houses, at the spot where the tarred road becomes unsurfaced path turn off left on a side track. This soon comes to a hydro-electric transformer station and, immediately afterwards, take a right fork up the hillside. After about 50 m there are cross-paths; turn right and you are on the main route, which is clear thereafter. The pipeline dominates the view as one wanders on through the jungle of birchwood. Last time there I found a dead slow-worm on the path, a casualty of a passing walker who had stood on it.

After 1 km or so the Allt na h-Eilde is crossed and it is then worth diverting upstream to see the waterfall though its flow can vary, depending on how much water British Aluminium are allowing through. Here too one can cut up the hillside to join another path which leads up this side valley, then climbs steeply up the prow of the Leitir Bo Fionn where the

---

Following the pipeline to the Blackwater Reservoir. The Aonach Eagach ridges beyond.

contouring pipeline/path from Loch Eilde Mor to the Blackwater is joined (see C, p 93 for this continuation). This prow gives a truly tremendous view to reward the toil up. (The riverside walk is the least panoramic route out of Kinlochleven.) From the Allt na h-Eilde bridge there are still 5 km to the dam and the path soon rejoins the river bank to follow it most of the way: pleasant, if unexciting, walking.

C. The Grey Mare's Waterfall

This is the most exciting way out of Kinlochleven even if it does start the day by climbing off in the opposite direction to the day's destination. Start from the centre of Kinlochmore where there are two park benches and a blue sign indicating the 'Gray Mare's Waterfall' or the 'Grey Mare's Waterfall', depending which side you look at! The UF church and surgery are passed, right, the police station, left, and at the T-junction St Paul's Episcopal church stands across the road with the waterfall path indicated beside it. (There is a car park and 50 m down the road a small grocer's. The church hall does tea or coffee.)

The way up to the Grey Mare's Waterfall is a good, made path. The fall can be heard well before it suddenly appears at a viewing point: a long plunge of water out of naked rock and, thanks to past lack of co-operation, this is the only river hereabouts not tapped and reduced in the BA catchment schemes. The Allt Coire na Ba drains a huge grassy corrie so there is usually a good force of water. The path continues, crosses a stream by a bridge, turns left, down the far bank, then curves round to the foot of the gorge, with the mighty torrent of the Grey Mare's Waterfall plunging into a high-walled cauldron. It is possible to boulder-hop/scramble right to the foot of the falls but the rocks are dangerous, being exceptionally slippery. Stott ranks the falls as being in the top half dozen in the country.

The 1:50,000 map shows two paths climbing up to join the Mamore Lodge—Loch Eilde Mor high-level road and these are both described. There are plenty of other paths and variants to mislead the walker and the complex succession of spurs and gullies, tree-clad, loud with falling waters, adds to the confusion. The path up towards Coire Ba has the finer views and is described first.

Backtrack from the Grey Mare's Waterfall to the bridge but, instead of crossing, keep on up the river bank and where the path crosses an old wall turn sharp left onto the path that leads steeply uphill. The view begins to open out at once as the path zig-zags up on the spur between the ravines, then the angle eases as the tree-line is reached. The view down Loch Leven is fine from here. The power line to the Lairig Mor passes overhead, then there is a forlorn gate and one comes out on to the open hillside. The path gradually swings left into the Ba glen (Mamore Lodge and the keeper's house are the white buildings across the valley) and a stream is crossed (small gate) then, shortly after, two more streams in a wooded hollow. The path then forks at a cairn and the right path is followed, first up the stream, then making a rising traverse up to the high-level road, where the route from

The huge Grey Mare's Waterfall in its secretive forest setting above Kinlochleven.

Mamore Lodge is joined (see below). Poucheresque views.
    For the more easterly path backtrack from the Grey Mare's
Waterfall, re-cross the bridge and return to the viewpoint
above the bank of this stream. There is a picnic table beside
the path and if one walks to it and on in the same direction
another made track is picked up (it breaks off from the route
up from the church at a bend 50 m before the viewpoint).
After a while this track forks, with a larger path heading right
and a smaller one left. Take the left fork, which immediately
crosses a stream, then turn uphill (a side path heads
downstream), and the route thereafter is unambiguous. One
passes under the power line at some ruins and then the path
runs up the crest between deep-set burns to gain the open
hillside above the tree-line. The high-level road is reached just
before its highest point. This path (an old stalkers' path)
crosses the road and curves away up to wend through the
eastern Mamore hills — a useful way to those summits. The
continuation for the Blackwater follows as described for a
start at Mamore Lodge.

D. The high circuit from Mamore Lodge

From Mamore Lodge the road bends round past the keeper's
house to the green valley of Coire na Ba (*the corrie of the
cows*, indicative of ancient grazings) and then rises steadily
round under the southern spur of Na Gruagaichean. The
views down and along Loch Leven become breathtaking.
About 1 km apart the paths from Kinlochleven, described
above (C), join the road. A watershed brings Loch Eilde Mor
in sight but before the loch is reached break off right on a
path which snakes down and across to the Allt na h-Eilde
where the pipeline is joined. The route of the pipeline is
shown with arrows on the map and on the ground is
paralleled by a track or path, a maintenance track to the spur
of Leitir Bo Fionn (*the slope of the cows of the Fionn*: a name
going right back into Celtic folklore) and an intermittent path
thereafter. Another route, up from the River Leven (B) joins at
this spur. Various deep-set streams slow progress a bit but
cutting corners does not help; keep to the pipeline till the dam
is reached.

The dam, almost 1 km long, 25 m high, was constructed between 1905 and 1909, one of the last big projects built with human labour. The reservoir created is 13 km in length. Previously there had been a few small lochs up the valley. Stories about the navvies abound, from mentions in Borthwick and other books, and more closely from Patrick MacGill's _Children of the Dead End_, which is autobio-graphical fiction, MacGill having worked on the scheme. For years after the dam was finished bodies and skeletons were found on the route over to the Kingshouse, the nearest pub. The drunken navvies would set off in the dark and be overwhelmed by blizzards or lost in mist — so watch out as you go. Below the dam is a pathetic group of gravestones, most with just a name, one is of a female, one just inscribed _unknown_. Life was hard (sixpence an hour and overtime till you dropped), there were horrific accidents, grim escapades but also a great hard-living companionship among the 3,000 Irish and Scottish navvies. Moleskin Joe, Carroty Dan and others became quoted cult figures of my youth. MacGill was a self-educated itinerant worker and his books have all been reprinted in Ireland or the UK recently. This wielder of pick and shovel described how one man hit a buried detonator and had his pick head driven through his throat. But he also wrote:

'All around the ancient mountains sat like brooding witches, dreaming on their own story of which they knew neither the beginning nor the end. Naked to the four winds of heaven and all the rains of the world, they had stood there for countless ages in all their sinister strength, undefied and unconquered, until man, with puny hands and little tools of labour, came to break the spirit of their ancient mightiness.'

There are two options for reaching the Kingshouse:

1. Bealach Lochan na Feithe

The pass through to Altnafeadh is obviously the easy option but the going can be on the wetter side of moist and there is no path. It is still a fine pass with only _c._ 70 m of ascent. The boggy nature of this route meant it was never used in ancient times when higher, drier ground was followed by humans and their cattle.

The Devil's Staircase zigzags above Alltnafeidh on the edge of Rannoch Moor. A view from the summit of the Buachaille: the Mamores and Ben Nevis in the background.

2. Meall Bhalach—Beinn a' Chrulaiste Pass

The going is rough, devious and wet in places when heading for the high pass east of Beinn a' Chrulaiste so gives a good test of one's route-picking and general navigation. The col itself is broken up by peat hags but the descent becomes much easier as one follows down by the Allt a' Bhalaich (*the burn of the pass*). The name implies no novelty in this route and contrary to parroted statements about 'not following streams', in wild, peat-ridden country this is actually the best line to follow. (The inane argument is that one might walk over a waterfall, which would demand a certain lunacy in the walker.) The going is often more practical by burns in peat country as old hands discover. In the great days of cattle droving a route came down 3 km east of the present Blackwater dam. There was a stance between two of the lochs now amalgamated in the reservoir and the beasts ascended by the Allt nam Fuaran (*the burn of the spring*), descended by the Allt Chailleach (*the burn of the old woman*) and so reached Kingshouse. They travelled from Fort William north of Ben Nevis and the Grey Corries to use the Lairig

Leacach, softer on beasts' feet than the Lairig Mor and Devil's Staircase.

Extra days at Kingshouse

Beinn a' Chrulaiste is a better hill than one might expect from a first view of it. There are three ridges, and all are good routes of ascent. My favourite is the NE Ridge; the special revelation of the view to the Buachaille and Glen Coe only comes as the summit flats are reached. The Buachaille takes on a ferocious jaggedness which would not be out of place in the Bregaglia and Bidean looks every inch the highest peak in Argyll. One expects great views on Corbetts; this one surpasses expectations. The NE Ridge can be climbed by those coming from the Blackwater dam, either returning to the col or descending the SE Ridge. Likewise routes to Alltnafeidh offer a traverse by the West Ridge, up, and SE Ridge, down. I've used all the ridges, and skied up, and ascended by exploring the crags — and I'd quite happily climb the hill again tomorrow: a great wee hill.

Meall a' Bhuiridh, 1108 m, is a much bigger proposition but an easy enough ascent. There is a fine view over Rannoch Moor, with Schiehallion beckoning the route ahead. The Buachaille Etive Mor is one of the great rock-climbing peaks of Glen Coe so should only be tackled in clear conditions or by the experienced. The popular 'easy' route is up Coire na Tulaich from Lagangarbh but it can also be climbed from the Glen Etive flank. The crags of Stob Dearg facing the Moor are the preserve of the climber.

The Kingshouse is reputedly the oldest inn in Scotland. It was a vital changing house and drovers' stance. From it coaches set off to cross the Devil's Staircase and cattle departed for the markets at Crieff or Falkirk or even London. Some notable travellers have left descriptions. In 1803 Dorothy and William Wordsworth (with Coleridge four days before them) came up through Glen Coe and Dorothy's journal painted a pretty raw scene.

> 'The first thing on entering the door was two sheep hung up, as if just killed, their bones hardly sheathed in flesh. After we had waited a few minutes a woman, seemingly about forty years old, came to

The Buachaille Etive Mor from Beinn Chrulaiste.

The Buachaille Etive Mor from the main road near Kingshouse.

us in a great bustle, screaming in Erse, with the most horrible peacock voice, first to one person, then another. She could hardly spare time to show us up-stairs, for crowds of men were in the house — drovers, carriers, horsemen, travellers, all of whom she had to provide with supper, and she was the only woman there.

'Never did I see such a miserable, such a wretched place, — long rooms with ranges of beds, no furniture except benches, the floors far dirtier than an ordinary house could be if it were never washed. We sate shivering in one of the large rooms for three quarters of an hour before the woman could find time to speak to us again; she then promised a fire in another room, after two travellers had finished their whisky, and said we should have supper as soon as possible. She had no eggs, no milk, no potatoes, no loaf-bread, or we should have preferred tea. With length of time the fire was kindled, and, after another hour's waiting, supper came — a shoulder of mutton so hard that it was impossible to chew the little flesh that might be scraped off the bones, and some sorry soup made of barley and water, for it had no other taste.

'After supper, the woman, having first asked if we slept on blankets, brought in two pair of sheets, which she begged that I would air by the fire, but behold! the sheets were so wet, that it would have been at least a two-hours' job before a far better fire than could be mustered at King's House, for the peats were not dry, and if they had not been helped out by decayed wood dug out of the earth along with them, we should have had no fire at all. The woman was civil, in her fierce, wild way. We talked over our day's adventures by the fireside, and often looked out of the window towards a huge pyramidal mountain, Buchal, the Shepherd of Etive. All between, the dreary waste was clear, almost, as sky, the moon shining full upon it. A rivulet ran amongst stones near the house, and sparkled with light: I could have fancied that there was nothing else, in that extensive circuit over which we looked, that had the power of motion.'

Charles Dickens travelled in the opposite direction. Rannoch Moor he described as being like 'the burial ground

of a race of giants'. Thirty-eight years had seen a change in
the King's House.

> 'When we came to a lone public called King's-house, at the
> entrance to Glencoe — this was about three o'clock — we were
> wellnigh frozen. We got a fire directly, and in twenty minutes they
> served us up some famous kippered salmon, broiled; a broiled fowl;
> hot mutton, ham, and poached eggs; pancakes; oatcakes; wheaten
> bread; butter; bottled porter; hot water, lump sugar, and whiskey;
> of which we made a very hearty meal. All the way, the road had
> been among moors and mountains with huge masses of rock,
> which fell down God knows where, sprinkling the ground in every
> direction ..... Now and then we passed a hut or two, with neither

*The Kingshouse Hotel on Rannoch Moor — the Creise Group of
hills above.*

window nor chimney and the smoke of the peat fire rolling out at the door. But there were not six of these dwellings in a dozen miles; and anything so bleak and wild, and mighty in its loneliness, as the whole country, it is impossible to conceive.'

The Moor has not changed, nor the setting of the hotel. Some of the windows give such splendid views that they are treated like pictures and have brass name plates on the sills. The hotel has had its ups and downs and now seems to be in need of considerable investment to overcome the wear of years. The bar is popular with weekend climbers. There are two houses offering B&B just along from the Kingshouse.

Accommodation: Rannoch Moor/ Kingshouse

The Kingshouse Hotel, Kingshouse, Glencoe, Argyll. 08556 259

Mrs Bennett, Corrieban, Kingshouse, Glencoe, Argyll. 08556 258

Mrs Ridley, Rannoch Edge, Kingshouse, Glencoe, Argyll. 08556 264

Kingshouse Hotel Bunkhouse (self-catering). 08556 259

Two possible alternatives for accommodation are Blackrock, 268531, and Lagangarbh, 221559. These are well-appointed climbing 'huts', belonging to the Ladies Scottish Climbing Club and the Scottish Mountaineering Club respectively. They are locked and only available to members of other clubs affiliated to the British Mountaineering Council or the Mountaineering Council of Scotland. Members should apply for using the huts through their own climbing club secretary, who should be able to supply current information.

As a last resort one could bus or hitch down to Glen Coe where the village has hotels, B&B, youth hostel, camp sites, etc, and return the next day. Or one could push on to Rannoch Station but that hard alternative should have been studied, planned and booked ahead and an early departure made from Kinlochleven. Rannoch Moor is not the place for an unscheduled bivouac!

Reading: Aitken, R.: *The West Highland Way*, HMSO, 1980.
Buchan, J.: *The Massacre of Glen Coe*, Peter Davies, 1933, reprinted, Buchan & Enright, 1985.
MacGill, P.: *Children of the Dead End*, 1914, reprinted, Caliban Books, 1985.
Prebble, J.: *Glen Coe*, Secker, 1966 (now in Penguin).

Day 7

Across Rannoch Moor

OS41, 42

This is one of the most serious days of the crossing and should not be underestimated. At the start of the day Rannoch Moor can lie benign and beautiful under spring sunshine yet a few hours later the wilderness may be swept by storms — a fearsome place. Given that sunny day the Moor has a crying beauty: glittering lochs, a rim of snow-limed, blue hills and the calling of the birds of the open spaces: skylarks, curlews, greenshanks, divers ... The name comes from *raineach* (a fern). The 'ferny moor' hardly sounds wild enough. The scale is big (most of mountainy Lakeland could be swallowed within its bounds) and the going is tough throughout. Dorothy Wordsworth noted how easy it was to underestimate the scale on Rannoch Moor but failed to do so in Glen Coe itself which she said was rather like parts of Lakeland. With Bidean rising to 1,150 m this was some underestimating. Rannoch Moor looks big — and is bigger still.

From Kingshouse cross the bridge heading north but where the road turns west towards Glen Coe turn east instead on a good estate road which is indicated Black Corries. This is a group of white, clean-gleaming buildings, hidden among protective trees and looking out over the Moor to the Achallader hills. About an hour's walk leads to them. Keep looking back for there are fine views to the Buachaille and the Clachlet hills.

Black Corries is typical of many isolated 'Lodges', built in the heyday of sporting estates. Their social position is perhaps questionable but the periodic outcry against stalking deer is often made for the wrong reasons. Deer have to be 'culled' in their own interests. They were originally forest animals and with Scotland's forests destroyed (centuries ago) have adapted to living in the harsher environment above the valley and such woods as remain. Forestry is protected by big fences to keep deer out. The over-grazing prevents any natural forest regeneration and given a severe winter or spring deer die of starvation in vast numbers. They are living in an artificial landscape (a man-made wet desert) and as such have to be 'managed'. The numbers to be culled have been worked out from years of research and the sadness is not that deer are shot but frequently not enough deer are shot and they suffer as a result. The anti-blood-sport lobby is frequently unaware of this situation. A bullet is a kindlier end than starvation. Stalking is often the only economic asset existing. (What else can you do with Rannoch Moor?) The hinds are shot after the stags, the work of the keepers not sportsmen and, whatever the set-up, the management of

A contrast:— Rannoch Moor in its winter splendor.

deer would have to be maintained.

Evidence of the original forest of Caledonia is clearly seen on the Moor where the bog-preserved flares of roots and branches stand out like bleached skeletons. The Moor is not all bog. There are green and grassy corners and plenty of ruins testifying to people living there in the past. Slithers of resinous bogwood made torches, spills and wicks for crusie lamps in olden times. Rannoch bogwood was sent all over the Highlands. Dorothy Wordsworth commented on the presence of bogwood:

> 'The ground... black and full of white bleached stones, pools as far as the ground stretched below us, perpetual traces of long decayed forest.'

Beyond Black Corries there is a much rougher estate road, as far as the old county march, and as this road wends in and out and up and down continually, allow plenty of time in any estimate. There is a further deterioration at a junction where one keeps to the right, the better left fork just going up to a TV mast. The road itself eventually dies in the bogs and it is very easy to go astray at this point as a decent path onwards is indicated on the map but is not there on the ground. There is no made path but only the markings of passing feet as they have traced out a bad path along the only feature, the line of wooden power poles. These in fact are a life-saver and in adverse conditions their line should be followed. The walking is often boggy and switchbacks continually so is both slow and tiring. Allow for this.

The views over Loch Laidon are superb and, given a good day, a picnic and swim off a granite-sand bay, is a delightful treat. Many of the islands are wooded as they are isolated from the browsing of deer, the moor's most numerous animal. The bird life gives a constant background music. A fascinating place. Tigh na Cruaiche is a ruined farmhouse which I first saw on a schoolboy crossing of the Moor in 1963, part of a heatwave walk from Killin to Skye, following The Road to the Isles. We left our camp near Rannoch Station at 5.00 am to break the back of the crossing before the desperate heat made walking nearly impossible. We brewed by these ruins after a swim in Loch Laidon. The Devil's Staircase was done at dawn next day but the Lairig

Rannoch Moor — evidence of its previous afforested state in the peat preserved tree stumps.

Sturdy Highland 'garrons' which are used for carrying dead deer and other loads where there are no tracks.

Mor was an oven. We plunged, fully clothed, into any stream and in half an hour everything was dry again. Rannoch Moor is never easy. Sometimes it is glorious. Sometimes desperate. But never easy.

The line of poles seems to go on for ever and there is a feeling of relief to top one more knoll and see Rannoch Station and the hotel in the distance even though a forest sprawls between. There is a dip and a rise up to a stile beside the gate into the trees. You are not 'out of the wood' however. The old right-of-way has been churned up by forestry vehicles and can be in an abominable state for walking. At the end of this steeplechase the route then swings up the hill (an unfriendly act for tired hikers) to become a proper forestry road. There is a signpost pointing back down the way indicating the route to Glen Coe. Deer can often be seen browsing the roadside and, early or late, in May, you may hear the strange bubbling call of the blackcock at their spring display, known as the *lek*. The path descends slowly to a gate/stile at the end of the forest and only a short swing of road remains up to Rannoch Station.

Rannoch Station is little more than the station and the Moor of Rannoch Hotel but always seems to bustle with people: train passengers coming and going, fishermen, walkers and tourists. It is not an easy place to photograph as there is an extraordinary clutter of poles and notices and the views out from it are too spacious and panoramic for most cameras. I find it a fascinating corner, whether reached

The lonely site of Rannoch Station on the Moor of Rannoch.

by car, train or, in our case, on foot. On the station platform is a tearoom offering homebaking and cooked snacks with a very friendly atmosphere. (Open Monday to Saturday 08.00–19.00; Sunday 10.00–19.00; tel: 088 23 209).

There are many stories attached to this station. On one occasion a train lost its guard's van on leaving Corrour and the van set off backwards. Corrour alerted Rannoch and the procedure called for it to be switched into a siding but with a guard on board they decided to let the van through instead. It came shooting out of the cuttings (one with our only real snow tunnel), and rattled over the high viaduct into and through Rannoch Station. Rannoch contacted Gorton, who let the runaway through. It finally came to rest beyond Bridge of Orchy! We once canoed across Rannoch Moor and turned

A view from the big viaduct at Rannoch Station: look out for it on the journey up to the start.

up at the station with six canoes. The station master did not know whether they should be charged by weight or length. He decided to weigh them and we dutifully carried the _lightest_ canoe in and out to the scales six times ... We also skated across the Moor and made use of crevasse-rescue ideas in case anyone went through the ice. Wearing life jackets and roped together was a novel combination.

Accommodation: Rannoch Station

The Moor of Rannoch Hotel, Rannoch Station, Perthshire, PH17 2QA; 088 23 238 is open April–November and occupies a crucial role in our crossing. It is a welcoming Highland hotel, but being popular with fishermen and walkers it is essential to book ahead as there is little alternative accommodation. Ample and delicious Highland fare will be welcomed by those who have crossed the Moor: bar meals or restaurant service. Hopefully there should be a new B&B near the station by now, otherwise the next B&B is 8 km eastwards: Camusericht Farm at the west end of Loch Rannoch. (It is the house beside the road and sleeps eight.) Contact Mrs Robertson, Camusericht Farm, Bridge of Gaur, Rannoch, Perthshire, 088 23 219. The hotel will always give helpful, up-to-date advice if they are fully booked.

It is probably worth emphasizing that this is the most crucial overnight stopping place of the crossing so it is worth booking here first, whatever date is possible, and working in the rest of the crossing before and after. Much the same applies to the Kingshouse on the other side of the Moor. One other possibility is to ensure reaching Rannoch Station in time to catch an evening train, either north (19.39) or south (18.48), or the post-bus (16.00) to Kinloch Rannoch, returning to Rannoch Station the following morning. The station has been going automatic/unstaffed for some years so for train times it might be safest to ring Glasgow 041 204 2844. Check the bus time by ringing 0887 (Aberfeldy) 20408 or 0796 (Pitlochry) 3333 or The Moor of Rannoch Hotel. The tearoom at the station is not affected by this change-over.

The Moor of Rannoch Hotel at Rannoch Station — a key stopping place on the crossing.

Camping Wild camping no problem at all. All Rannoch Moor is available!

Extra days at Rannoch Station

Rannoch Moor can be a terrible place in bad weather but it also has an extraordinary fascination and beauty. You may well want to linger, doing nothing and resting afterwards or taking in extra walks and hills. By using the train a good tramp back to Rannoch Station is possible and several hills are near enough to offer sport.

There is another advantage here. Rannoch Station stands on 300 m, which is a useful proportion of whatever height has to be climbed to a summit. Western hills are much more demanding in this respect. Dr Johnson made this observation too, a rather long-winded observation, the outcome of theory rather than practice.

'The height of mountains philosophically considered is properly computed from the surface of the next sea; but as it affects the eye or imagination of the passenger, as it makes either a spectacle or an obstruction, it must be reckoned from the place where the rise begins to make a considerable angle with the plain. In extensive continents the land may, by gradual elevation, attain great height without any other appearance than that of a plane gently inclined, and if a hill placed upon such raised ground be described, as having its altitude equal to the whole space above the sea, the representation will be fallacious.'

Heading north by train, descend at Corrour and walk eastwards to Loch Ossian, with its attractive view, then take a rising path up to join the old 'Road to the Isles' route which swings round Carn Dearg's slopes past the ruins of Corrour Old Lodge and down to the Allt Eigheach. From there an estate road leads out to the B846 at Loch Eigheach, $2\frac{1}{2}$ km east of Rannoch Station. Resist the temptation to cut the corner back home — the ground is punishingly boggy. Maps 41 and 42 cover this walk. Using the train both ways to Corrour, Beinn na Lap (Munro, above Loch Ossian) and Leum Uilleum (Corbett, SW of the station, much the finer hill) are good summits for a between-trains day. They are both on sheet 41. On sheet 42, north of Rannoch Station, is a fine circle of hills drained by the Allt Eigheach, which gives a good anti-clockwise traverse: over Beinn Pharlagain (Meall na Meoig is a Corbett), Sgor Gaibre and Carn Dearg (both Munros), and back either down the Coire Eigheach path or off Sron Leachd a' Chaorainn to the Corrour path.

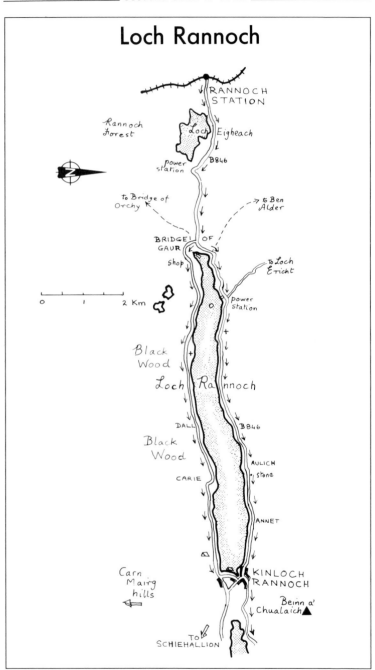

Loch Rannoch

RANNOCH STATION

Rannoch Forest

Loch Eigheach

Power station

B846

to Bridge of Orchy

to Ben Alder

BRIDGE OF GAUR

Shop

to Loch Ericht

Power station

0   1   2 Km

Black Wood

Loch Rannoch

DALL

B846

Black Wood

AULICH
stone

CARIE

ANNET

Carn Mairg hills

KINLOCH RANNOCH

Beinn a' Chualaich

To SCHIEHALLION

Day 8

Loch Rannoch

OS42

There is a choice of routes for walking along Loch Rannoch and though I've walked and explored both north and south shores I would not like to advocate one or the other. Both are described as objectively as possible so you can decide for yourself. First there is the 8 km down by Loch Eigheach and the River Gaur, miles which take the walker from the wild spaciousness of Rannoch Moor to the rich forests and farmlands of Loch Rannoch.

Loch Laidon and the waters of Rannoch Moor (their springs up on Clachlet almost on the western seaboard) drain by the Garbh Ghaoir into Loch Eigheach, 2 km east from the hotel. Heading north from the road is a track, indicated by a right-of-way guidepost, saying 'Road to the Isles' (ideas for future treks!), which leads through by Corrour and Loch Treig to the Lairig Leacach (mentioned on p 68) and Spean Bridge. This junction marks the old drovers' stance so predates the railway which only opened in 1894. The road drops more steeply to cross the Allt Chalder and, looking back up the Gaur, there is a small dam and power station which makes use of this drop in height. There is a very long fish ladder, worth seeing if interested in Hydro structures. You can cross below the dam and follow down south of the River Gaur to Rannoch Barracks and Bridge of Gaur but much of the going is rough and untracked. The road itself keeps on along the north bank, an unusual area of scores of bumps covered in boulders of all sizes, dumped by a huge glacier in times past.

Left *The fish-ladder at the power station on the River Gaur.*

Below *Highland Cattle enjoying the summer sun.*

At the junction 501571 the decision has to be made: to walk the north shore, the *slios min* (the side of gentle slopes) or the south shore, the *slios garbh* (the side of rough slopes). Both are very attractive, the north shore with much birch wood and the classic view of Schiehallion, the south shore with the great Black Wood of Rannoch. One friend so enjoyed the one shore that next day he took the morning bus to Bridge of Gaur in order to walk the other shore. He too refused to name a favourite side.

Clach na h-Iobairte near Craiganour Lodge on the north side of Loch Rannoch.

A. North shore

Just past the junction is Camusericht Farm, which offers B&B as mentioned above. Rannoch Lodge is roofless but has a certain prominence on one day a year when there is a race from Rannoch Lodge to Kinloch Rannoch — swimming! In the corner the track goes off to Loch Ericht, 'the old sawmill track' to us as youngsters, leading to Ben Alder bothy and plenty of cross-country expeditions. Over the next 2 km there are some stretches of sand along the shore and gentle views up the loch. The road north to Loch Ericht at Bridge of Ericht is locked, the gate with spikes on top and if anything detracts from the north shore it is the plethora of prohibition notices. Visitors are hardly made welcome. Rannoch Power Station does not win any beauty competitions but the view over the loch is good. The little island with the tower is described later. The water for the power station comes from Loch Ericht.

Killiechonan is just a scattered hamlet. An old walled graveyard just before the burn is overgrown. The commonest name on the stones is Macgregor; there are many Stewarts as well; Camerons; Menzies, etc.

The next landmark is Talladh-a-Bheithe Lodge, now a German-run licensed guest house/café, open Easter–October. The cafe may be more than welcome. Their brochure warns 'We are specialised in homebaked German Cakes'. The next 5 km runs through superb woodlands: mostly birch and oak on the north shore, the light greens a contrast to the darker Scots pine forests on the south shore. Rannoch has given its name to three species of moth: Rannoch Brindled Beauty, Rannoch Looper and Rannoch Sprawler. The first was discovered in 1871 but the specimen lost. Re-discovered some years later the collector celebrated to such an extent he could not find the location again. Eventually it was found again by someone who was not a lepidopterist.

The policies of Craiganour interrupt the trees, fields made out of another alluvial estuary. Clach na h' lobairte is a hatchet-shaped standing stone above the road. Aulich is the site of an old 'bloomery' where iron was smelted using local wood which had been turned into charcoal. Each furnace used 120 acres of trees a year and such was the forest destruction that parliament had to pass an act protecting native trees. Vast acres were burnt to reclaim fields or free hiding places from robbers and wolves.

The next 2 km gives Rannoch's most classic view: Schiehallion at its most graceful, framed by the silver birches and mirrored in the calm loch. I just hope that is how it is for you for the view really is one of the best of the crossing and much better than calendars and biscuit tins make out. At Annat an old right-of-way heads north over the hills to join the A9 at Drumochter. Where the track crosses the Annat Burn there is a whole village in ruins. Locals point out a big tree as the Gibbet Tree where a cattle thief was hanged in 1754, and a house further on bears the name Chemical Cottage. At the Loch Rannoch Hotel (an ugly time-sharing complex) there is a standing stone called Clach na Mharsain (*the packman's stone*) which marks an unfortunate accident. A packman, an itinerant pedlar selling ribbons and buttons, scissors, chapbooks and such items along the Highland roads, sat down for a break and rested his pack on top of the stone. The pack slipped off and the strap caught him round

Schiehallion, across Loch Rannoch.

An oddly-named house on the north shore of Loch Rannoch.

the neck — and strangled the unfortunate fellow.

The shore where the road turns into the village saw a sad shipwreck in 1983. After a great deal of difficulty enthusiasts raised the *Gitana*, a 30 m steam launch which had sunk in the loch in 1882 only a year after being launched. The *Gitana* was originally transported in sections and put together again at Kinloch Rannoch. Unfortunately there are no sheltered anchorages on the loch and a storm smashed the windows so the launch swamped and sank. After 100 years submerged her raising was a notable event. *Gitana* was in remarkably good condition but before restoration could begin there was a similar storm and she broke loose to be smashed on the shore at the entrance to the village. Kinloch Rannoch is an odd name for the village. Kinloch means *head of the loch* (as in Kinlochleven) so why does it apply to a place which is at the foot of a loch?

B. South shore

Turning off for the south side of Loch Rannoch one comes to a charming corner. The river, broad and deep, winds round past Rannoch Barracks (a trim mansion on the site of the old military post) and under a graceful bridge (1888), the whole area richly green and graced by beautiful trees. Little touches of magic like this spot can be completely missed by the motorist. The Post Office/shop (shut Wednesday, Saturday and Sunday) is passed, then the small school, then the smaller Braes of Rannoch Church up on the right. Gleann Chomraidh leading away to the SW, is another old drovers' way, often known as the Thieves' Road, which leads over the edge of Rannoch Moor to Bridge of Orchy, the route now largely taken by the railway.

The road returns to the shoreline at Finnart Lodge for 3 km of birch wood. Out in the loch there is a small tower built on an island barely larger. This is Eilean nam Faoileag (the *island of gulls*) a prehistoric man-made island or *crannog*. Many lochs in the central Highlands have *crannogs*, several with secret causeways or stepping stones leading out to them. (This one is so linked to the south shore.) They are amazing structures to have lasted a thousand years and what of the skills that could drive great piles into the water and fill them with rocks and wood and soil? The MacGregors sought refuge on this island (now often just called Tower Island) and twice at least they were destroyed by punitive raids. The Robertsons imprisoned a raiding MacDougall chief on the island and when the jailors brought the weekly food supplies they were always careful to leave a guard on their boat. One day the captive purposely spilled a sack of apples and in the general scramble to retrieve them even the guard joined in. And the captive rowed off! Loch Rannoch is rather lacking in real islands, two delta remnants (Gaur, Ericht) being all there is. There is another small *crannog* off Finnart.

Camghouran's open fields and scattered houses indicate the site of one of the many ancient villages round the loch. Unobtrusively sited across some fields the cemetery shown has grim associations. The stone left of the gate is Clach-na-Ceann (*stone of the heads*) where five Cameron children were brained by their mother's jealous lover. Many other Camerons came to be buried here over the years so the graveyard is often called the Cameron Graveyard rather than St Michael's.

The next 3 km leads along the edge of the Black Wood of Rannoch, a magnificent area of old Scots pines now carefully maintained by the Forestry Commission. In spring or autumn the mixture of birch and pine colours is magnificent and the verges are a mass of delicate ferns, primroses, wood anemones, blaeberries and other flowers. The waters lap mere yards away and across the loch the slopes rise up to Beinn Mholach. After the Dall Burn is crossed there is another open area, the playing fields of Rannoch School, the main building of which, the old Robertson house of Dall (later owned by the Wentworths) stands back behind rows of yew trees. Few schools can have such a pastoral setting. The school was founded in 1959 on the Gordonstoun model. Paths from Dall and Carie combine to cross the hills to the south to Glen Lyon. Known as the Kirk road it was the route many clansmen were carried over to be buried in home territory. 'Coffin roads' such routes were called.

Carie, 2 km further east, has a car park and several laid-out walks in the forest. Rannoch Forest covers a huge area, besides its heartland of the old Black Wood. The Munros to the south are rather bleak, boggy and bare on the Rannoch

side, a contrast to the green slopes and corries of Glen Lyon.
The conifers give way to deciduous trees for the last 2 km
of the lochside walk. Beinn a' Chuallaich behind Kinloch
Rannoch dominates the view to the NE, its ascent perhaps
reason enough for an extra day here, even if the larger
temptation of Schiehallion did not exist. The road forks at the
end of the loch. Cuilmore and Bunrannoch House lie along
the right fork (see below); the village is reached along the left
fork, passing the conical cairn of the war memorial on the
way. It looks right up the length of Loch Rannoch. The small
village lies on both sides of a bridge which arches over the
outflow of the loch, a friendly place and the centre of life
round Rannoch and Tummel. The marble monument in the
village is to the local evangelist, teacher and poet Dugal
Buchanan who died in 1763.

Extra days at Kinloch Rannoch

Beinn a' Chuallaich is invisible from Kinloch Rannoch but
Craig Varr, a spur of the hill, is the prominent feature
overlooking the village. The Allt Mor tumbles down into the
village and a path (and track) zig-zags up through the woods
beside the *big burn*. Start at the gate just beyond Brown's
garage. Once above the wood you can traverse along above
the trees to Craig Varr or just wander up by the Allt Mor over
the moors, by either route eventually ending at the big cairn
of Corbett Beinn a' Chuallaich, *hill of the herding*, which
offers a sweeping view in all directions. The words of the
tramping song *The Road to the Isles*: 'By Tummel and Loch
Rannoch and Lochaber I will go' take on a new meaning
when the eye can survey those named places and know they
have been *walked*. The view south is dominated by
Schiehallion (*the fairy hill of the Caledonians*) and this may
well be where the extra day will go, the lure of the big at
work. The view from Schiehallion is not as fine and the
ascent is much less interesting.

People are rather directed into climbing Schiehallion from
the Braes of Foss car park (752556) which is fine if you have
a car. Carless in Kinloch Rannoch may decide one to make a
more direct ascent. A lift to the car park and walking back
over the mountain is one ploy. A slight diversion at the Foss

start lets one see a cup-marked stone (752553), a mysterious prehistoric survival. There are scores of these pock-marked stones and some have rings round the hollows ('cup-and-ring stones') but why they were made is quite

The old mansion of Dall, now Rannoch School — on the south shore of Loch Rannoch.

Beinn Chuiallaich above the east end of Loch Rannoch

unknown. The track by the Tempar Burn to Gleann Mor and Fortingall is an ancient route out of Rannoch. Gleann Mor is full of ruined shielings, the good grazing a reflection on the presence of a belt of limestone. Fortingall has two claims to fame: a yew tree which is undoubtedly the oldest living thing in Britain and a claim, of some dubiety, to be the birthplace of Pontius Pilate.

Accommodation: Kinloch Rannoch

Dunalastair Hotel, Kinloch Rannoch, PH16 5PW 08822 323

Bunrannoch Hotel, Kinloch Rannoch, PH16 5PU 08822 367

Bunrannoch House, Kinloch Rannoch, Perthshire 08822 407

Mrs A Steffen, Cuilmore Cottage, Kinloch Rannoch, PH16 5QB 08822 218

Mrs Legate, Glenrannoch House, Kinloch Rannoch, PH16 5QA 08822 307

Both hotels are huge so accommodation should not be a problem. Local questioning usually turns up other B&Bs in the village. Bunrannoch House and Cuilmore lie along the right fork as one reaches the end of the loch. Bunrannoch was once the home of Auchinleck, the soldier, and is a tall building with superb views. Cuilmore can be a unique overnight stop in that Mrs Steffen offers outstanding gourmet meals. Dinner and breakfast are likely to be recalled as highlights of the crossing. The house stands in a flowery garden, they grow all their own fresh vegetables, have a variety of livestock and the cottage itself is fascinating. Booking is essential and it is worth phoning a few days beforehand to discuss the dinner menu!

The energetic might like to walk on 5 km of tomorrow's route to stay at the Home Farm, Dunalastair, Kinloch Rannoch, PH16 5PA, 08822 387, where Mrs Kennedy offers DB&B (712596).

Camping The Bunrannoch Hotel also operates a conveniently sited camping ground next to the hotel and there is a Forestry Commission site at Kilvrecht, 616565, the entrance 1 km east of Carie (Forestry Commission, Kilvrecht, Lochend, Kinloch Rannoch, PH16 5QA. 08822 335).

Shops Wednesday is early closing day but the Country Store is open then and 10.00–13.30 on Sundays in summer.

Loch Rannoch mail bus J. M. Duncan, Kinloch Rannoch. 08822 348. Departs 07.30 and 13.30 for Rannoch Station.

Reading Ratcliffe Barnett: _The Road to Rannoch and the Summer Isles_, Edinburgh, 1946.
Cunningham, A. D.: _A History of Rannoch_, Rannoch, 1984.
Cunningham, A.D.: Tales of Rannoch, 1989.

Tummel

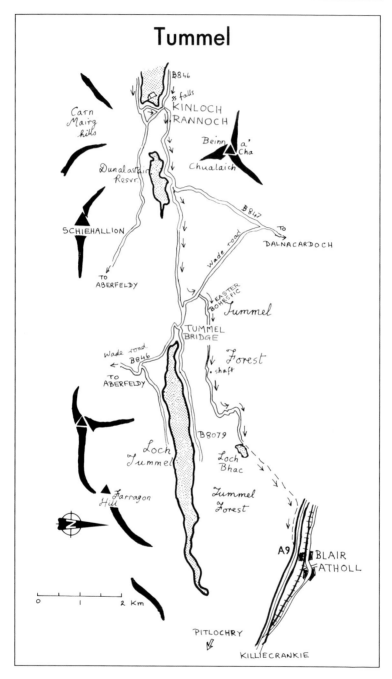

B846
falls
KINLOCH
RANNOCH
Carn
Mairg
hills
Beinn a'
Cha
Dunalastair
Resvr
Chualaich
B847
TO
DALNACARDOCH
SCHIEHALLION
Wade road
TO
ABERFELDY
EASTER
BOHESPIC
Jummel
TUMMEL
BRIDGE
Wade road
B846
Forest
TO
ABERFELDY
shaft
B8079
Loch
Jummel
Loch
Bhac
Jummel
Farragon
Hill
Forest
N
A9
BLAIR
ATHOLL
0   1   2 Km
PITLOCHRY
KILLIECRANKIE

Day 9

To Blair Atholl

OS42, 43

A varied but easier day which, like yesterday's, makes plenty of eastings. If you have not already done so do have a look at the rushing waters of the Allt Mor before leaving the village. Opposite Brown's garage is Allt Mor Crescent, where the 'Riverside Walk' is picked up — a pleasant path alongside the

Schiehallion from the road along by Dunalastair Reservoir.

river. After an open space cross the B846 to a gate and track signposted 'Hillside Walk', which takes one up above Drumchastle Wood, with grand views of Schiehallion, and then drops back to the road at Drumchastle Cottage: a very pleasant kilometre.

Schiehallion continues to dominate, viewed for the next stretch across Dunalastair Water, a marsh-edged reservoir. The road is a succession of bends but the traffic is unusually well-behaved and the odd idiot can usually be heard well in advance of his appearing. Drumglas, a house up on the slope above a bay, has a colourful May–June display of rhoddies etc. The B847 branches off for Trinafour, linking up with Wade's road north from Tummel Bridge. Shortly after there is a short, sharp rise with a bad bend, the extra height serving to expand the view even further. Schiehallion begins to fall back and the Farragon summits lie ahead. (Howe Farm, north of the road, does B&B.) Visible, down in a gorge, is a weir where an aqueduct bears off the water for the Tummel Bridge power station but enough of the flow remains for the river to rush on in a series of rocky falls. Motorists cannot stop and few even notice this wooded ravine below the twisty road.

After a big bend the road is straighter past the coldly tidy house of Dalriach. You can follow the river bank for a while again or be tempted into brewing by the river. Keep an eye open for chickweed wintergreen, *Trientalis europaea*. Regain the road in time to turn left at the junction, 753595, which is the Wade road north and which sweeps up the hill with military directness. After 1 km turn right into the Tummel Forest on the Easter Bohespic forestry road. Bohespic means *bishop's dwelling* and is mentioned in a charter of 1515. There were six settlements between Tummel Bridge and the Bohespics and as recently as 1820 there were nineteen houses at Over Bohespic and six at Easter Bohespic.

Now Easter Bohespic is a mere croft, isolated among the massive acres of forest. A gate leads into the forest and the road climbs steadily for 1 km when it joins another, better, forest road. Bear right at this junction and after another 1 km there is an opening with some marvellous panoramas: right back west along Loch Rannoch to the hills on the far side of the Moor, across to Schiehallion (a different shape now), down to the Tummel Bridge Power Station, and out to the knobbly Tummel summits of the Farragon hills. Have a look at the shaft shown on the map. It is found half-hidden above the road and one can set the echoes ringing inside.

Some dedicated tramping follows, the road being rather hedged-in with the trees, but there are glimpses of the view and some bright areas of primroses. A junction is reached, eventually (798603) but be careful, it is right on the edge of the map and the turning may be missed. The junction is clear and our route turns steeply uphill, with a wall on its east side. A forestry sign even points out 'Loch Bhac', our immediate destination, and a site worth reaching for a picnic lunch, even if it may be a bit late.

The road runs straight, with a backward view to Farragon Hill, then swings right, still climbing but not so steeply. Sheet 43 shows various footpaths crossing and looping the road but these are not all that clear on the ground and should be ignored. Ben Vrackie sticks out occasionally to the east, above the trees. When the final rise is reached there is a sudden view to the great Glen Tilt fault and the lumpy array of the Beinn a' Ghlo hills. The road now begins to drop steadily towards elusive Loch Bhac. I call the loch elusive because several friends have had trouble finding it but there shouldn't be any real difficulty.

A flat, quarry-like opening on the right warns of the impending criss-crossing of roads and paths which causes the confusion. Ignore everything and shortly after, on the left, is a car parking area with another Loch Bhac sign and also a sign prohibiting cars to proceed any further. Take the indicated Loch Bhac track (between posts) and soon after crossing a wee burn this barely motorable track swings right to end at the loch beside the Pitlochry Fishing Club facilities. Loch Bhac has been a favourite brew spot for many Ultimate Challengers as well as fishermen. The shallow waters give a good paddle and the encircling trees relent at the far end to stand back and reveal the Beinn a' Ghlo hills again. Relaxing there on one crossing I quoted Dr Johnson to the girls: 'We were in this place at ease and by choice, and had no evils to suffer or to fear'.

Finding the path out of the trees has also proved difficult. Leave the lochside as you reached it but, in less than 100 m, as the track swings left break off from the bend rightwards into the trees on a footpath which is none too visible to start. Once found it runs clearly enough through a narrow ride in the trees and leads to a stile over the forest-edge fence. A solitary old iron gate stands by the fence like some forgotten sculpture. The path, beyond the stile, almost at once crosses a small stream and bears off right (ignore a left fork from the stream) to begin its long steady descent over big heather moors. The path is usually clear, so long as various sheep tracks are left alone, and runs steadily to the NE, gradually losing height and drawing close to the birch-clad depths of the Allt Bhac. This route is shown on several maps, one as early as 1725 showing it as part of a 'road' linking Inversnaid Barracks on Loch Lomond with Ruthven Barracks near Kingussie.

The track wends through the trees, partly sunken here, partly worn by tractors, goes through a gate, then swings right and down to another gate opposite Balnansteuartach (a decaying mill wheel can be seen on the building). This gate is slid across and then can be opened enough to go through. Ensure it is closed again properly. One debouches onto the farm drive. Turn right and wend round up to the farm, passing through another gate *en route*. Before reaching the farm bear left by the lime trees to more gates which allow access to a farm track which runs along between fields: basically two ruts in the grass, but initially fenced on both sides, then only on the right. Just keep to this track. Blair Castle, white and clear, is straight ahead.

The track descends almost to the buzzing A9 then runs along through the fields just above this busy road. All the interconnecting fields are used for lambing and dogs should never be taken through this way. The track undulates across several open fields, drops to a burn and ends at a gate onto the A9. There is a stile beside this and one across the dread A9. Crossing this race track is probably the most dangerous part of the whole coast-to-coast route. Over the second stile there is a small gate leading to a lane which twists down to a footbridge over the River Garry. A right-of-way, signposted for Tulach Hill and Fincastle comes in too. Across the Garry the walker is turned left to come out onto a street which leads up past the restored water-mill to cross the railway to reach

Brew time by Loch Bhac — the Beinn a'Ghlo hills now in sight.

Blair Castle — home of the Dukes of Atholl, a welcome landmark by the A9.

the old A9. The Old Mill has a tearoom with delicious home-baking — a most welcoming first stop in Blair Atholl. Various milled grains are on sale too and you can wander through the three storeys of the mill and see it working.

Blair Atholl (*the plain of Atholl*) was built in its entirety as part of the Atholl Estates. The policies lie east of the village and the castle grounds are rich parklands, sometimes used for events like Scout Jamborees. There is an extensive luxury caravan and camping site. Facing the site entrance is the Atholl Country Collection, a display of local life and lore (including a blacksmith's smiddy), housed in the old school.

The Atholl Estates have been blessed by an early duke being a tree enthusiast (an early grower of larch in Scotland) and by the fact that limestone runs through the area; these two factors combine to give Blair Atholl its unusual green lushness.

Blair Atholl is, strictly speaking, the village north of the River Tilt. The larger village south of the bridge is Bridge of Tilt and outwith the Atholl estates. Old Blair lies up behind the castle, the original route through the Highlands going that way and, now, the new A9 is on the other side of the River Garry.

Having arrived (probably) in late afternoon there will not be time to explore Blair Atholl's main interest, Blair Castle. This certainly deserves a visit and one answer is to visit the castle the next morning, then walk down to Killiecrankie and on to Pitlochry for an evening at the theatre and staying overnight in the town — thus adding a fascinating day to the crossing.

Extra days at Blair Atholl

Blair Castle

The castle is reached up a magnificent avenue of lime trees (which buzzes with bees in season) and flanked by green fields, on the right given over to the camp site, on the left to the occasional Scout Jamboree or such special events. Even without a romantic castle the Atholl estate shows what can be done in the Highlands, though the unusual underlying limestone is a great help.

The first mention of the castle was in 1269 when the Earl of Atholl complained to Alexander III that John Comyn of Badenoch had made an incursion into Atholl and built a castle. The main tower is still called Cumming's (Comyn's) Tower. The earldom reverted to the crown and was then bestowed on James II's half brother and when the Stewart male line ended, it was transferred, by marriage, to the Murrays. Cromwell held, rather than destroyed, the castle and in the Williamite period Atholl supported the new king. Dundee had taken and garrisoned the castle when he had to move off to meet the government army at Killiecrankie. Being on the right side was rewarded, the earl became a duke. In the Fifteen rising the duke supported the government but his heir, the Marquis of Tullibardine, and his brothers Lord Charles and Lord George Murray were 'out'. (Nothing like backing both sides!) Lord James, second son, succeeded to the title and in the 45 we had the ironic situation of one brother defending the castle and another attacking it, in what was the last such siege in these islands.

Over thirty rooms are open to the public and a visit to the castle is a real walk through history. Some odd traditions remain. The duke, with more titles than any other peer, is the only person allowed to maintain a private army. As boys camping in the grounds some of us were shown round by a charming elderly man who we later discovered was the duke himself. The present duke is a very distant relative (you go back seven generations to find a common link) and, being a bachelor, the next duke will be another distant cousin. At one time the Dukes of Atholl inherited the sovereignty of the Isle of Man (which was sold to the Crown in 1830). The odd inheritance game is well illustrated in this tenacious family.

The Beinn a' Ghlo hills

This 'hill' is a group of several hills (3 Munros) and can give a good day's outing from Blair. The easiest approach is to follow the small tarred road up to Loch Moraig and then the estate track which wends on towards Shinagag. Head up Carn Liath (_grey cairn_) first, then traverse Braigh Coire Chruinn-Bhalgain (_the slope of the bag-shaped corrie_), Airgiod Bheinn (_silver hill_) and Carn nan Gabhar (_cairn of the goat_). The easiest return is to go back to the col to the _braigh_ and descend southwards to the Allt Coire Lagain valley and so back to Loch Moraig, or go on to Shinagag and down the Glen Girnaig (fine falls) to Killiecrankie. The descent into Glen Tilt is very steep and the river often unfordable — not a recommended return route.

On the other side of Glen Tilt Carn a' Chlamain (_kite's cairn_), Beinn Mheadhonach (_middle hill_), and Beinn Dearg (_red hill_) are Munros or Corbetts of interest which stand on the edge of the wild, empty, boggy, 'Ring of Tarf'. Beinn a' Ghlo means _hill of the weather_ and the weather in the end decides whether we want to add hill days to the crossing.

Relief as boots come off — at Laggan Guest house in Blair Atholl.

Accommodation: Blair Atholl

Most of the Blair Atholl B&B houses are situated in the Bridge of Tilt area, down St Andrew's Crescent or on The Terrace. From the Glen Tilt Hotel walking southwards there is a butcher's shop on the right, at the corner with St Andrew's Crescent. The Terrace lies at its termination. Mrs O. Stephen, Laggan Guest House, has proved a friend to many walkers (evening meal too), but below is a list of all the places I've noted. There are two hotels; both provide bar meals and a full range of accommodation.

Glen Tilt Hotel, Blair Atholl, PH18 5SU. 0796 81 333
Atholl Arms Hotel, Blair Atholl, PH18 5SG. 0796 81 205
Mrs O. Stephen, Laggan Guest House, The Terrace, Bridge of Tilt, PH18 5SZ. 0796 81 269
Mrs A. Campbell, Arrochar, The Terrace, Bridge of Tilt, Blair Atholl, PH18 5SZ. 0796 81 228
Mrs H. Gerar, The Firs, St Andrew's Crescent, Blair Atholl, PH18 5TA. 0796 81 256
Mrs J. Andrews, Invergarry Guest House, Bridge of Tilt, Blair Atholl, PH18 5SZ. 0796 81 255
Mrs D. Herdman, Woodlands, St Andrew's Crescent, Blair Atholl, PH18 5SX. 0796 81 403
Mrs MacDonald, Beechwood, The Terrace, Bridge of Tilt, Blair Atholl, Perthshire. 0796 81 379

Camping There is a luxurious site in the Blair Castle grounds (expensive for small tents) but the site signposted behind the Glen Tilt Hotel does not take tents.

Reading *Walks; Pitlochry and District*, Pitlochry Tourist Association leaflet.
Kerr, J.: *Wade in Atholl*, Blair Atholl, 1986. *Old Roads to Strathardle*, Blair Atholl, 1984 (These studies may be available in the Atholl Arms or Blair Castle.)
Blair Castle: Illustrated Guide (available at the castle).

White foxgloves — not uncommon in the Highlands.

Blair Atholl to Kirkmichael

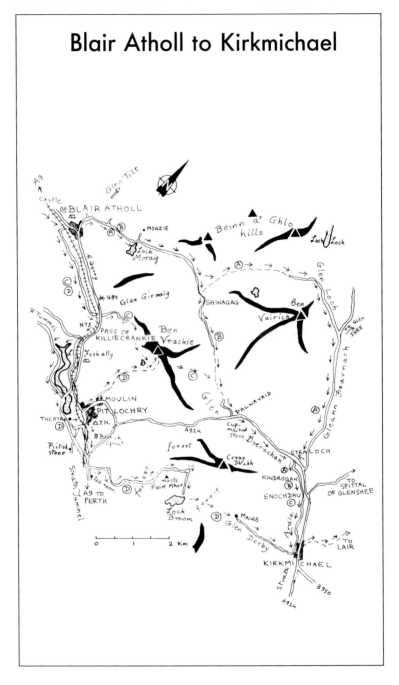

Day 10

Blair Atholl to Kirkmichael

OS43

Today offers more choice of route than usual for several ancient tracks and drove roads link the Great North Road of the A9 with quiet Kirkmichael in Strath Ardle. A. The Glen Loch road which is, 3–4 km apart, all minor tarred roads or estate roads; B. The old road to Glen Brerachan, shorter, with a 6 km hill pass; C. To Killiecrankie and over Ben Vrackie, a demanding hill day with road walking to start and finish; D. Going via Killiecrankie and Pitlochry (extra night) and then easy moorland walking. These are described in turn. There is also an option of heading to the Spittal of Glen Shee (see p 165) instead of Kirkmichael, a route which initially follows description A before branching off.

A. The Glen Loch road

Take the road up the east bank of the River Tilt (opposite the Glen Tilt Hotel) to Old Bridge of Tilt which, originally built in the sixteenth century, was the only crossing on the Tilt and later part of the great road north. Turn right just before the bridge (signposted for Glen Fender) and for the next 2 km keep in low gear for the 'stey brae'. There is one fork, well signposted, and we bear right for *Monzie 2*. (There is also a Right-of-Ways Society sign pointing to *Strathardle*.) The road twists up to a world of vivid greens for there is an area of intrusive limestone to contrast with the normal browns of the acid peat moors. Marble was once quarried in Glen Tilt and the name Marble Lodge is still on the map. The Tilt is an extraordinary fault line, with many kilometres of steep, V-shaped slopes, leading through to Deeside and beyond.

As we gain height the symmetrical cone of Carn Liath (*grey cairn*) is seen ahead. Beinn a' Ghlo is the collective name for the three bold Munros of this group but they are best left for a day to themselves. (Carn Liath alone would add ± 3 hours to the day.) The public road ends just beyond gull-noisy Loch Moraig where a gated farm road breaks off from the Monzie track to head over the moors under Carn Liath. This is our route. The track goes on to Shinagag, a deserted shepherd's house, the last occupant having been murdered (after retiring elsewhere!). Behind Shinagag is the pass to Glen Brerachan, described under B, and this is well seen from the highest part of the road under Carn Liath.

In wet weather we cross to Shinagag and take the track northwards but in normal conditions this corner can be cut. Where the Shinagag road drops SE from Carn Liath's slopes (939683) there is a rough vehicle track bearing off left, beside a small gravel pit, and this wends on over to the Allt Coire Lagain — just the time and place for a paddle and making tea. Last time I crossed there, with two girls, the

A study in symmetry — Carn Laith of Beinn a' Ghlo.

stove was just going when I noticed a very agitated sandpiper scolding us. Sure enough, a few feet away, was its nest of speckled eggs. We moved, in bare feet still, to picnic further up the burn.

The path on the map is not so clear on the ground but the pass, between Beinn a' Ghlo and Ben Vuirich, can hardly be missed and just over the crest of the pass an estate road is picked up. Ben Vuirich is not much to look at from the pass but is a superb viewpoint and worth taking in before descending into Glen Loch. The initial slopes are a bit wet and one has to walk round the summit plateau rim to see the panorama. The days ahead are well displayed. See if you can see the sea! Vuirich means *roaring* or *howling*, in this case of wolves, of which the hill had more than its share in the past.

A tiny hut at the foot of the steep descent (994717) can offer emergency shelter. Please leave no litter. At one time the country north to Loch Loch had many shielings for summer pasturing cattle and led to feuding between Atholl and neighbouring estates. Mary Queen of Scots attended a great deer hunt when over 2,000 beasts had been herded together (the work of 2,000 men over two months!) and these were being driven to the Loch Loch camp when the Queen ordered a dog to be loosed on a wolf. This startled the leading stag and the deer stampeded into the herding Highlanders who only had time to fling themselves on the ground before the deer thundered past. Several were killed.

By the loch is Cumming's Cairn which commemorates the unfortunate clansman of that ilk who had been surprised at a wedding feast at Blair Castle and had to flee up Glen Tilt. Two of the pursuers cut over behind Carn Liath and lay in wait by the loch. Big Cumming paused to rest and was lifting a hand to wipe his sweaty brow when his enemy fired. The arrow pinned his hand to his forehead.

The road rather wanders for 3 km down Glen Loch to Daldhu at the junction with Gleann Fearnach. (The Glen Shee route turns up here; see p 165 for the continuation of the description.) There are 8 km of track down Gleann Fearnach, and they can feel more, for the glen is rather featureless and bleak. When the Allt Fearnach and the Brerachan Water meet they become the River Ardle and, as if by magic, there is a change to rich green fields and forests. When the A924 is reached turn *right* up through the hamlet of Straloch which is little more than a church, a school and a couple of houses. Look back behind the buildings on the north side of the road and you'll see an old lime kiln. The loch lies in a secretive hollow. At West Lodge we cross to head for Kirkmichael down the west side of lush Strath Ardle. Routes A, B and C all go this way so, for the route from West Bridge to Kirkmichael, see p 140 under C.

B. Shinagag—Glen Brerachan

There are two ways one could reach the historic pass through to Glen Brerachan. The first follows route A (Glen Loch road) as far as Shinagag, the second comes up Glen Girnaig from Killiecrankie, using part of route C and is described shortly.

Shinagag is a secretive setting guarded by large sycamore trees. The whole area from here to Blair Atholl was once heavily populated (well documented in John Kerr's booklets) and in some places the only indications of past habitation are solitary sycamores. Glen Girnaig is full of sad ruins or abandoned houses. At Shinagag 200 years ago stood 35 buildings, three kilns, mills and an inn.

Shinagag means *the old pass* and the route is of historical importance (Kirkmichael once had a big fair) and is shown as a road on Roy's map of 1755. Mary Queen of Scots, in 1564, came through to Shinagag and down Glen Fender to Blair Castle so that choice has a certain royal precedent. Very little of the 'road' can be seen now and paths (see OS 1:25,000 sheet NN 86/96) are not always clear on the ground, or, in contrast have been overlaid by recent rough vehicle tracks. Considering the knobbly roughness of the hills this pass between Ben Vrackie and Ben Vuirich is surprisingly open and direct.

Waterfall enthusiasts might like to follow route C (page140) as far as Killiecrankie but instead of cutting up for Ben Vrackie they can continue by Druid and a bulldozed track up Glen Girnaig to reach the Girnaig Falls (925650): a straight drop in dramatic surroundings, a fall deserving to be better known. Continue up the east bank to the Allt a' Mhagain confluence (if in spate conditions footbridges at 927653 and 928655 allow a bypass) where a track climbs to pass Loinmarstaig and on up the Allt a' Mhagain. Cut along above this abandoned house on a track which leads to the ruins of Reinakyllich. At the burn before the ruin turn eastwards below a craggy knoll to gain the pass from Shinagag.

From Shinagag go through the gate beyond and, from the first wee rise, bear right: the track aims for the trees shown in the mouth of the pass. (There is another plantation, not shown on maps, in the NE corner of this big field.) Beyond the trees a bulldozed track is picked up and followed through the pass. Drop down to the Allt na Leacainn Moire thereafter. The river flows through a flat hollow so was always easy to ford when this was a well-travelled road.

This was the site of Riecharlotte which had ten buildings and kilns in the 18th century. A nearby gravestone marks a winter mishap long ago. A party bearing a coffin from Glen Brerachan were caught by a blizzard here and had to abandon their charge to seek shelter. They were not able to return for six weeks and then decided the deceased had grown accustomed to that spot anyway so he was buried there instead.

Ath nam Breac (*speckled ford*) is named only on the 1:25,000 map but at 978652 there are still plenty of shieling ruins in the green turf dominated by a big boulder.

There are old gates on each side of the river from more recent fencing. Cross the river and begin a rising traverse to pass just below the crags of Crungie Dubh (the 988644 summit). Look back for a fine view through the wide pass to Carn Liath.

On the 'old road' from Shinagag to Glen Brerachan — the pull up from the ford at Ath nam Breac.

The strange cup-marked stone in Glen Brerachan. The building is Dalnavaid.

A close-up of the cup-marked stone in Glen Brerachan.

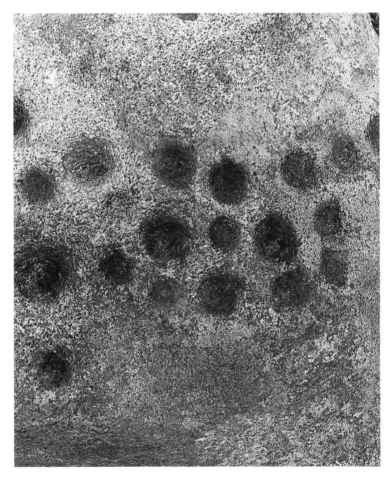

There are no signs of the old road until the crags are reached, then a track becomes evident as it wends up to cross the saddle between Crungie Dubh and Balgholan Craig to the secretive glen beyond. Follow the track down to cross the stream and curve round to the corrie lip where the old road is suddenly very clear, wending steeply down like an ancient sunken lane. In places it is overgrown or messy from modern use but is still an impressive bit of engineering. The road slopes down to follow along above the head dyke then, through a gate, angles down across a field to Stronhavie, a derelict farm with some massive trees. Descend to the A924 where it has been re-aligned, leaving the old bridge standing aside.

The cup-marked stone shown on the map is a fine example and worth finding. Walk up towards the telephone box and through the gate to pass behind the cottage of Dalnavaid. The stone lies at about the same level, 200 m along, on the slight spur, 30 m from the top fence of the field.

The farm of Dalnacarn (*field of the cairns*) is probably the site of a notorious inter-clan battle for in the nineteenth century coins of that vintage were turned up and many slabs and cairns destroyed in agricultural improvements. The story is worth telling as a typical example of Highland feuding and regal ineffectiveness.

Duncan the Fat of Atholl had married one of his sons to the daughter of the laird of Glenesk, in Angus. Another daughter of the laird was married locally to Sir David Lindsay. Both lassies were richly endowed but the Duncansons claimed they were cheated by Lindsay and a typical feud ensued between the Atholl and Angus families. A meeting was arranged to settle the matter but Atholl did not turn up and a son of the Wolf of Badenoch urged them on to raid Lindsay instead. The fiery cross went round and soon the Duncanson rabble burst into Angus bent on plunder. Sir David Lindsay had fought a combat *à l'outrance* on London Bridge before Richard II so was quick to react. Mustering sixty men he rode round by Blairgowrie to catch the raiders in the rear and somewhere in Glen Isla near mount Blair there was a bloody fight (1389). The Atholl raiders numbered 300 and eventually inflicted a heavy defeat on the Angus men before bearing off their booty. The Duncansons were 'put to the horn' but hid successfully in Atholl where they were to become Clan Donnachie (the Robertsons), but the Wolf's son was caught and executed. Lindsay determined to raid into Atholl as retribution but the Atholl men heard of his coming and set out to meet him. The Highlanders of Atholl prevailed again over the Angus men in the battle fought in Glen Brerachan. In 1396, before the king, came the bloody 'staged' fight on the North Inch of Perth, which was intended to stop not only this feud but all such squabbles. However, central government often found the clans beyond their control in the centuries ahead.

C. Over Ben Vrackie via Killiecrankie OS43, 52

Ben Vrackie, *the speckled hill*, is conveniently climbed from the northern end of the Pass of Killiecrankie — the hardest route to Kirkmichael. As the route from Blair Atholl to Killiecrankie is also the start for one approach to the Shinagag — Glen Brerachan road, route B (p 136) and also for the walk on through to Pitlochry, route D (p 145) that description is given first.

Blair Atholl to Killiecrankie

Cross the River Garry by the footbridge (yesterday's arrival point) and turn left, downstream, along a minor road for 4 km of rich river bank walking to the gorge of Killiecrankie. The road becomes progressively better but there is no traffic worth mentioning apart from that going to or from the limestone quarry above Shierglas. The quarry is hardly noticed and the buzz of the A9 fades once the new road crosses to the other side of the Garry for its high-level route through the gorge. There are snowy, scented bird cherries in plenty in May–June and cowslips and other wild flowers crowd the verges under the fine trees. On the slopes across the river the fateful Battle of Killiecrankie was fought in 1689.

The Pass of Killiecrankie is one of those places where geography and history have, perforce, clashed throughout time. The great road north had to come through its gorge and the railway and the new A9 have followed, century by century. The River Garry still churns its way through at the bottom of the wooded gorge and the grandeur and wildness are hardly affected by even these major intrusions. The gorge is now in the care of the NTS and footpaths link it and the River Tummel riverside walks with those round Loch Faskally (see p 148/154). Our quiet road crosses the start of the gorge by a high bridge built in the 18th century along with the Garry Bridge near the south end of the pass. The Garry Bridge had one arch and, alongside it, a circular hole which could relieve pressure in spates. This bridge is something similar but the extra opening is not quite circular as it is on the bedrock of the bank. As the old Garry Bridge has gone have a look at this one before going on, over the railway to join the ex-A9 at the hamlet of Killiecrankie (Post Office/shop). We then pull up a brae past the Killiecrankie Hotel to the NTS visitor centre.

Killiecrankie and its battle

The visitor centre has an interpretative display, a book and souvenir shop, toilets and a snack bar (hot pies or ice cream can be equally welcome!), so is worth a visit, even if the pass itself is not going to be followed. The pass saw plenty of action as a result of the battle. King William's commander General Mackay led his men through its difficult terrain and they were still forming ranks when Viscount Dundee (Graham of Claverhouse) swept down with his Highlanders. It was as much a rout as a battle but in that irresistible charge Dundee himself was mortally wounded. The Jacobites won a singular victory but thereafter, leaderless, soon lost the campaign. (At Dunkeld a few months later Mackay had his revenge.) Robert Burns wrote one of the most tingling atmospheric songs of battle about 'the Braes o' Killiecrankie, O'. I noticed cards with the words were on sale at the visitor centre. A few incidents of the battle are mentioned on p 146. William and Mary were crowned in 1689, the same year as the battle.

Ben Vrackie Traverse

From the NTS visitor centre walk north up the old A9 towards the first bend where a small tarred road branches off, signposted to Old Faskally. Take this: twisting up under the new A9 road and past a house and the gates of Old Faskally. Keep on the tarred road until nearing the farm, then turn off right and, shortly after, left over a cattle grid to go up beside a shelter belt of conifers. Starting with the cattle grid there must be half a dozen types of barrier to be faced (a gate that lifts, a kissing gate, and so on) before the open hillside is reached. Every gate is different. At the top end of the trees bear off on the right fork, round the top of the field and through a gate. A couple of minutes later turn up and back, left, onto a lesser track to a gate at the top of the field. (The road onwards ends at two small reservoirs.) Go through the kissing gate and along to finally leave the cultivated land by a gate through the hill dyke.

The track zig-zags up heathery pasture to an old wall and a gate in a fence just beyond, then bears right across the open hillside, crossing the Allt Eachainn, the burn that drains this corrie dominated by Ben Vrackie's summit cone, before heading up the hill opposite in another series of bends, clearly seen from below. Also visible from below is a footpath bearing off left as the slope steepens. This is followed through the heather towards the pass, goes over the saddle of a dark heathery prow and, 200 m beyond, one is on the pass looking down on Loch a' Choire. The tourist track from Pitlochry/Moulin (described on p 157) crosses below the dam of the loch and makes a brutal assault up the peak. The steep track can be seen from the col so skirt north of the loch to join this. If heavily laden, the rucksacks can be hidden out of sight and the final ascent made more freely. This is perhaps the best ploy anyway as the direct route off the summit of Ben Vrackie (Ben-y-Vrackie as the locals say) is over very knobbly country.

Ben Vrackie has a huge view that ranges from Ben Nevis to the Cairngorms, to the near Beinn a' Ghlo group, from Schiehallion and Lawers to the hills south of Edinburgh. In some ways it is this open spaciousness to the south that makes the view special. Being like a nose thrust out from the Highlands Ben Vrackie frequently catches a blow of weather. Vrackie translates as _speckled_ and often enough has a dappling of cloud while Pitlochrie (old spelling) lies in sunshine.

From the summit descend the NE Ridge and then turn down easily enough to the col to Carn Geal. Descend to the north of Carn Geal, initially avoiding the boggy corrie, then following down near the stream draining it. One can descend on grass all the way. This burn is shown bifurcating, a very unusual feature, which you can check out on the ground. Cross the Allt na Leacainn Moire and angle up the hillside to the SE. As this is the line of the old road from Blair Atholl via Shinagag to Glen Brerachan and Kirkmichael it is described under B on p 137.

On UC 88 we returned to Loch a' Choire and headed generally SE to reach the A924 Pitlochry–Kirkmichael road but this line is very wet initially, gave wearisome thrashing through deep heather and an extra 4 km of tarred road. One could more pleasantly go over or round Carn Geal to a footbridge (sheep bridge) at 986631 and then down the Brerachan Water, with its attractive falls, to a sheepfank and track along to Stronhavie. One could also descend by the 'tourist route' to Pitlochry, have an evening at the theatre, and reach Kirkmichael the following day (see p 159). These hill routes are not advisable in the shooting/stalking season.

Just before the 384 m highest point on the Pitlochry–Kirkmichael road there is a memorial stone like a big milestone. Erected 'by a few friends', the inscription reads: 'In memory of John Souter who perished here in a snowstorm, 3rd March 1897'.

Glen Brerachan is, initially, a rather bleak glen with a few farms and rocky crags on its north side. A richer landscape is reached just before Gleann Fearnach comes in and Strath Ardle is attractive throughout its length. We turn off the A924 over the bridge at West Lodge and walk down to Kirkmichael on the west side of the strath. Dowan is a farm/mill which has been converted into houses and the 1700 mansion of Kindrogan is now a popular field centre offering a wide range of courses and natural history holidays. (Information: Kindrogan Field Centre, Enochdhu, Blairgowrie, Perthshire, PH10 7PG. 025 081286.) The house, a range of white buildings, stands in attractive woodlands, the home of many rabbits and red squirrels. After the East Lodge is passed there is a beautiful old three-arched bridge (a listed building) which leads across to the hamlet of Enochdhu (Post Office/shop).

Strathardle: the trim old building of Kindrogan, now a busy field studies centre.

There is a crude new forestry bridge as well. A right-of-way sign indicates two miles to Kirkmichael which is a bit of an underestimation. Keep to the rightmost road which swings round a bend to Dalreoch farm. Leave its buildings to the right and, just past them, the track forks, each fork with a gate. Take the right gate and the track curves up to a field which is crossed to the plantations ahead. Gate, stile and waymark post indicate the start of a clear path through the trees. There are gates and stiles at one place in the middle and one comes out at a small loch (left) with a white cottage south of it. One joins the road from Loch Cottage and this wends on to Kirkmichael which, latterly, can be seen ahead. The landscape and the small village are most attractive.

On one heatwave crossing our route from Blair Atholl via Killiecrankie and over Ben Vrackie to Kirkmichael proved a bit much for the senior lady of the party and she nearly passed out at dinner in the Strathlene, thereby missing one of the best meals offered on the trip. The Strathlene is an old coaching inn (tastefully modernized), right in the centre of the village, facing the old humped bridge and church, and has a well-deserved reputation for good food. Kirkmichael accommodation, see p 164.

If going direct Blair Atholl to Kirkmichael, the following

The hamlet of Enochdhu in Strathardle.

Pitlochry notes are irrelevant. Day 11 is described on p 171.

D. By Killiecrankie and Pitlochry
OS43, 52 (adding a day)

The walk from Blair Atholl to Killiecrankie has already been described under route C, p 140. This continuation is highly recommended if the extra day can be spared. Ben Vrackie can still be traversed and possibly enjoyed all the more for being such a contrast to the richness of the countryside round Pitlochry. And there is the chance of a night out at the Festival Theatre. Keep up the contrasts!

Killiecrankie to Pitlochry

There is a plethora of paths between Killiecrankie and Pitlochry but the following is what I consider to be the most rewarding combination. The scenery is all arboreal richness and as one gazes out over genteel Loch Faskally it seems hard to believe lonely Loch Loyne or Loch Laidon on Rannoch Moor belong to the same planet. There are various descriptive leaflets in the NTS visitor centre and on the outside wall, facing the road, is a large-scale map which is very useful. With so many paths there can be some confusion but most vital junctions or car parking access points are well signposted or have a map board. You may stray but cannot really become lost.

Pass on beyond the map display to the start of the path; it is well signposted and there is a letter box in the wall to the right. The path dips into The Troopers' Den where a slatted footbridge takes one over the burn, with an interesting view *under* the road to the right. The path curves round above the *den* and descends various steps and zig-zags to a turning for the Soldier's Leap. The Troopers' Den recalls the first casualty of the Battle of Killiecrankie when a Highland sniper fired from across the pass and brought down one of the horsemen. The Soldier's Leap records a remarkable escape. A soldier, Donald MacBean, in a desperate bid for safety leapt the river which here narrows to a cut about six metres wide: a feat few would care to emulate without such ultimate motivation.

Walk along the main path southwards. The railway which we walked over on the descent (safe it its tunnel underfoot!) now comes out to stride across the foot of the Troopers' Den in ten graceful arches, part of Joseph Mitchell's great railway route to the north, completed in 1863. Even a bridge for a burn has a decorative turret. On a bit, look out for a stone on the path which is indicated as marking the spot where Brigadier Barthold Balfour of the Dutch Brigade, who commanded Mackay's left wing in the battle (1689) met his end in the rout that followed. The path is like a tunnel through the trees and it is hard to believe the railway and two roads are tiered up the slopes above. There is a wishing well on the left. Eventually the path joins a stretch of tarred road (a milestone notes 'Blair Atholl 3' and 'Tummel Bridge 11') and leads to a tubular footbridge but, if one looks carefully, the signs of the old Garry Bridge to Strathtummel can be seen. This was akin to the bridge we crossed at the north end of the gorge but had one big arch and the overflow completely round. Those bridges were not old, being built in 1770.

The Garry Bridge replaced a ferry and (sounds familiar) it took a ferry tragedy when eighteen people drowned on the way back from Moulin market before the bridge was built.

Right *The splendid entrance hall of Blair Castle* (From His Grace the Duke of Atholl's Collection).

Below *The visitor centre at Killiecrankie, a welcome mix of interpretation display, shop and refreshments.*

The stark modern lines of the Garry Bridge at Killiecrankie.

The only survivor of the tragedy was the boatman who was yanked out by his wife using a boathook. The bridge was built by public subscription. It collapsed in 1955, a demise forecast by the shadowy figure of Thomas the Rhymer. The scale of the gorge is well seen from the footbridge and the new Garry Bridge downstream is simply a stroke across the sky, 'graceless utilitarian'. I can recall a temporary Bailey bridge across the Garry and the bad turning off the A9 down to it. Now this bridge is our footpath.

One can stay on the left bank and walk on to Pitlochry (see p 154), but our route crosses the bridge and goes down the right bank. The path splits just short of the new, high bridge, the right fork going up to a car park, the left, as indicated, passes under the new bridge and on for the 'Linn of Tummel'.

The path splits again, the route right climbing up the hillside to a viewpoint before descending again to rejoin the lower path. The lower path is the one I'd suggest following south along the River Garry to its junction with the River Tummel (which is also the upper end of Loch Faskally) and then west up beside the Tummel, an area exclusively planted with larch trees which glow orange and gold in the autumn. The Linn of Tummel was once the Falls of Tummel but, with the creation of Loch Faskally attacking its foot and a curtailed flow of water coming down, the glory has departed. The rocky gorge with its rough cascades is still bonny however.

By a post numbered '6' there is also a sign for the Coronation Bridge but before turning right, upstream, as indicated, take the path straight on to the water's edge.

There is a small obelisk commemorating a visit from Queen Victoria in 1844. Stott (*Waterfalls of Scotland*) quotes Swinburne's 'roguish' comments about this somewhat phallic stone, and lists the many authors and painters who dutifully came to marvel at the falls, which are just out of sight from the monument but they can be reached by

Crossing the Coronation Bridge over the River Tummel.

crossing the nearby footbridge. The footbridge crosses the
remains of an old salmon ladder (build a century ahead of the
Hydro one at the other end of Loch Faskally) and one can
only marvel at the 'prodigious labour' to hack this out of solid
rock. For half its length it runs through a tunnel.

Continue up the path by the Tummel. There are several
viewpoints of note and then a suspension bridge allows one
to cross to the other bank. The Coronation Bridge commemorates the coronation of King George V and Queen Mary. The
route now follows the minor road (Pitlochry to Foss via the
south side of Loch Tummel); this wends along above the
River Tummel and Loch Faskally in very pleasant fashion. A
sign indicates the Falls of Tummel and a footpath descends
to the river there. Continue along the road which leaves the
woods to curve round above the Clunie Power Station. The
water driving its turbines comes by a tunnel from Loch
Tummel (which is dammed — Clunie Dam — at its eastern
end) and the memorial arch at the power station entrance
shows a cross-section of such a hydro tunnel. This is our
third day of walking through the catchment area of the big,
complex hydro system and the exhibition at the Pitlochry
dam is well worth a visit to see just how big and complex the
scheme is.

Note, on the right, as we continue what the map calls
'Chapel Stone'. Older sources call this the 'Priest's Stone'. It
is an old cross slab, rather weathered and overlaid with
lichens, but worth scrambling up the bank to see.

The road, traversing high above Loch Faskally gives wider
views. The loch is an artificial hydro-scheme one, created by
the construction of the Pitlochry dam. Being in such a touristy
area the hydro works have been well engineered and
landscaped and many pleasant walks round and above Loch
Faskally have been laid out. Just before more trees close in
on the road there is a specially fine view northwards over the
loch and through the Pass of Killiecrankie to the Beinn a' Ghlo
hills.

The buzz of the A9 is soon heard and the highway bridges
dramatically across Loch Faskally in one giant stride. (A cairn
on the north lochside path bears a Saltire Aware plaque for
the builders of the bridge.) There is an iron footbridge arching
across the loch as well which, though it looks older, was only

The Clunie Arch above Loch Faskally — a monument to local hydro works.

built in 1950 to replace one which used to cross the River Tummel before Loch Faskally was created. If desperately thirsty there is a small cafe at the boat-hiring hut in the bay just across the bridge (cross the bridge and turn right for 200 m passing the Saltire cairn), otherwise pass under the A9 and up a straight section of road. As it bends to join the A9 turn left (signed for Pitlochry Dam) and go through a gate for a bit of old road through a self-sown wild garden, gold with broom early and scented with honeysuckle in high summer.

A path breaks off right, through a gate, to wend along by the busy A9 but keep to the route (signed for the dam) which drops down steps back to the lochside. The view is to Ben Vrackie above the trees across the water. The dam is soon reached and can be crossed to Pitlochry but, better still, turn down by and over the salmon ladder to spend some time at the dam's attractions. The double loop of the ladder is interesting and an observation room has been created so one can actually see through glass panels into the water. Salmon-spotting is the name of the game. A fish-counter records an average of 5,400 salmon passing up-river in a year. The stretch of river below the dam is a favourite with anglers, at least with anglers who don't mind having every cast watched by a comment-passing audience!

The dam is described as a 'concrete gravity dam and

Boats for hire lie in a quiet corner of Loch Faskally near Pitlochry.

The Festival Theatre at Pitlochry.

coverwall 1,671 ft long, 57 ft high' and 65,000 tonnes of concrete were used in its construction. The rotating parts of the two Kaplan turbines weigh 93 tonnes. From late March to late October there is an exhibition in the visitor centre at the dam and anyone with any interest in hydro-electric schemes will find this fascinating. There is an audio-visual presentation and a range of publications is available at a bookstall. Outside the door are sample trees, labelled with descriptions, to help tourists recognize the forest trees round the loch.

From the dam a short walk downstream leads to the Pitlochry Festival Theatre. This has a magnificent setting above the river, looking over Pitlochry to Ben Vrackie and, besides the evening plays there are café facilities and the Brown Trout Restaurant and a regularly changed display of paintings. It is my favourite theatre anywhere, though I'm certainly a biased enthusiast, having been a regular visitor since schooldays when John Stewart, the founder, kindly showed me round and gave me dinner before the performance began. The theatre was then housed in a big tent and run on faith. The present building still has something of an open-air feel to it with huge glass windows looking over the river to the hills. And the atmosphere is friendly. Recently I watched a hiker leave his rucksack in the booking office and tramp in, big boots and all, in cheery conversation with a party in evening dress. The 'canvas theatre' was founded in 1951, but the marquee eventually succumbed to a gale and in 1953 another tent was erected with a semi-permanent structure. Semi-permanent proved to be about thirty years. Prince Charles opened the present splendid building in 1981. (The old one still survives as a curling rink.)

The theatre season runs from early May to early October. Brochure from Pitlochry Festival Theatre, Pitlochry, Perthshire, PH16 5DR (0796 2680). The coffee shop opens on 1 April.

Just downstream from the theatre is a green suspension bridge (Port na Craig Bridge) which gives access across to Pitlochry. This unusually long footbridge was 'erected in memory of Lt Col Sandeman of Fonab' and 'opened by the Marchioness of Tullibardine on Empire Day 1913'.

Before crossing however there is one interesting feature to see at Dunfallandy, 1 km to the south. Take the main exit from the theatre and turn left then, when this road turns to cross the Aldour Bridge into Pitlochry, keep straight on along the minor Logierait road. The Dunfallandy Stone is signposted: up a flight of steps on a tree-covered knoll, outside a graveyard. This is a Pictish symbol stone and they are described more fully later (Meigle Museum p 188) but if you visit this one you'll be intrigued I'm sure and want to see more. One side is framed by two serpents and bears a central horseman of beautiful simplicity. Above are two seated prelates facing a cross and scattered throughout are seven of the mysterious symbols: crescents and V rods, two 'swimming elephants' and others. The other side has a big ornate cross and ten animals, realistic or symbolic and two 'angels' which may be eastern gods! In its shelter the stone is nearly impossible to photograph.

Return and cross the suspension bridge near the theatre rather than use the vehicular bridge beside the caravan park. Once across, a road beyond twists up to the town centre. Do pop into the station. On the up-platform is what has been called the country's 'most beautiful Victorian cast-iron fountain'. Pitlochry's setting has largely been responsible for its popularity and as a walking centre it has plenty to recommend it. A 'What's On' publication can be obtained from the tourist office (see below). Pitlochry was spelt Pitlochrie originally and the prefix *Pit* is an indication of Pictish origins though, before Wade's road north, Moulin was the more important place. Pitlochry boomed with the coming of the railway in 1865, helped by the praise of the Queen's physician. (The 'hydro' survives as a baronial hotel.) There is a story of a local laird going to London to consult Sir James Clarke about his health and being recommended to take a holiday in the salubrious atmosphere of Pitlochrie.

Killiecrankie—Pitlochry by east side of Loch Faskally

Instead of crossing the Garry footbridge walk on down the left bank and under the high-level motor road. A path follows close to the river with one sortie inland, where a path breaks off for the Faskally Home Farm camp site, and a Pitlochry sign points back along the river which, almost unnoticed,

A superb cast—iron fountain at Pitlochry railway station.

becomes loch. The Clunie Power Station lies across this narrow end of Loch Faskally then, on our side, there is the imposing Victorian mansion of Faskally House, backed by some superb trees. The house is now a Strathclyde Regional Council outdoor centre and beside it are the freshwater fisheries laboratories of the Ministry of Agriculture, food and Fisheries. Follow their drive round a bay but, when it rises inland, turn off through the trees by the loch, where there is quite a confusing number of paths. With the loch on the right and the roar of the A9 on the left you can hardly become lost however. This Dunmore Forest has some fine trees and a secretive loch in its heart.

One comes out onto an unexpected bit of tarred road that has no continuity inland and Loch Faskally is on the other side. This oddity is explained at the viewpoint by the loch where a plaque explains the platform is built with some of the masonry of the old Bridge of Clunie which crossed the Tummel here before being demolished in 1950 with the construction of the hydro works. The old bridge was built in 1832 from money raised by public subscription.

The number of bridges and ferries past (and present) can be quite confusing. The hydro replaced the old bridge with the Clunie footbridge which we come upon round the corner, right below the huge, high span of the new A9, and also the vehicular Aldour Bridge at the downstream end of Pitlochry — so there are two for the price of one. The Clunie footbridge was the first in the UK to be constructed of aluminium alloy.

Round the corner, having passed under the A9 bridge, is a friendly cafe and boating centre. Follow the drive up by the Green Park Hotel, which hogs the waterside, and either walk in to town by road or, at the end of the hotel's policies, cut down again to the lochside for a footpath along to the dam. The path continues from the dam down to the Port-na-Craig footbridge below the Festival Theatre.

───── Accommodation: Pitlochry ─────

As Pitlochry is a major tourist town with over 100 listed hotels, guest houses and B&B facilities (and plenty others not listed) it is impossible to list them all here. Apart from

July and August pre-booking is not essential. The Pitlochry and District Tourist Association's Centre, 22 Atholl Road, Pitlochry, PH16 5BX (0796 2215/2751) will make bookings for B&B (in person or by phone). They also issue an accommodation register each year and, if one wants to be certain of accommodation in advance, this is worth sending for. The information centre is open all year.

There is a Grade 1 youth hostel: Braeknowe, Knockard Road, PH16 5HJ (0796 2308) with 78 beds. Booking is advised in July and August and on holiday weekends. The hostel is signposted clearly from the town centre and is just five minutes up the hill — so it commands extensive views over the town.

Camping is not so convenient. The only site taking tents without a vehicle is at Faskally Home Farm, PH16 5LA (0796 2007), south of the Pass of Killiecrankie (915603). I seem to recall a B&B nearby boasting of being the most central house in Scotland. We certainly feel far from the western sea. The Milton of Fonab site south of the town is only a caravan park.

Taxis Pitlochry (0796) 3333, 2454, 2290, 2516.

Reading Dixon, J. H.: *Pitlochry Past and Present*, Pitlochry, 1925 (very valuable, with fascinating photographs).
Several booklets about Killiecrankie (the battle, nature trails, etc) are available at the NTS visitor centre.

Over Ben Vrackie to Kirkmichael
OS52, 43

Everyone locally calls the hill Ben-y-Vrackie but I'll keep to the OS name for convenience. Walk up the A924 Kirkmichael road (Bonnethill Road, then West Moulin Road) to the old hamlet of Moulin, which at one time was larger than Pitlochry itself. Turn left on the small road behind the historic inn (signposted). This swings right then turns sharply left. At this bend take the rougher minor road straight on up, past Balemund, to a small car park among the riverside trees. The path is clearly indicated and is followed up through pleasant birch and pine forest to the start of the moors. A stile crosses the deer fence at the top of the tree line and the path can be seen running on through the heather to go through a gap between craggy hills. On the way up the view to the south has a special feeling of spaciousness and a commemorative bench indicates one family's devotion. I give details in my book *Climbing the Corbetts* but, briefly, the bench is a memorial (erected by a Perth family) for their son who was killed in a road accident in Australia. A few winters ago a tractor slipped on the icy hillside and was only saved by the bench stopping its slide down the hillside.

Through the gap Loch a' Choire suddenly comes into view with the steep final craggy upthrust of the Corbett beyond. The path climbs steeply, to the right of the crags and is clearly seen from below. There is a revealing view of the Highland hills as one reaches the top. A view indicator helps to work out the confusion of hills in view. The indicator is a memorial to the Leys School, Cambridge, which was evacuated to the Atholl Palace Hotel during World War 2.

Don't underestimate Ben Vrackie. An isolated position ensures it catches more than its share of storms. You can leave Pitlochry in sunshine and be battered by a blizzard on top, even in mid-summer. The Souter memorial at the

Ben Vrackie seen across the Moulin Moors.

summit of the A924 is a reminder! The various descent lines from the summit are described under the traverse of the hill (C, p 143).

Over the moors to Kirkmichael
OS52 or 53

Drovers used to come over from Kirkmichael by Glen Derby and Loch Broom to Ballinluig (on the way to Crieff market) and as Pitlochry grew at the expense of Moulin, routes from Pitlochry made basically the same crossing to Kirkmichael. Unfortunately there has been a great deal of commercial conifer planting on the moors and the old routes have been obliterated as scant attention was paid to the needs of walkers or old rights-of-way. This is a pity as the country round Edradour is some of the most scenic in the Highlands. As it is only 20 km to Kirkmichael there is no need to rush this day and the longest walking route outlined should be taken, even if it begins with 100 m of the ascent being lost again. This route takes in the romantic Black Spout waterfall and Edradour where, scenery apart, there is 'Scotland's smallest distillery'. Alternatives, cutting out Edradour or Edradour and Black Spout are also given.

Walk along the main street (Atholl Road) but where this swings under the railway to become the Perth road turn left onto Knockfarrie Road. The gates of the Atholl Palace Hotel are on the left. A sign on the right declares 'Black Spout 1 mile'. Walk up the road past the houses (two do B&B) and on by the hotel service road, then branch off on the first footpath, right. There is a sign and it does say 'Black Spout' — but on the back of the board where it can't be seen! This path leads down to, and along, a burn (the Kinnaird Burn), and at the next fork keep right. There is a confusing notice indicating the hotel's private gold course but once over the footbridge there is another 'Black Sprout' sign. Go uphill for 100 m and, when the path splits, keep to the left fork which leads on through a splendid area of oakwood. Scotland is rich in oakwood and many areas of the old, original woodlands must have been like this. It was not all dark pine trees. Oak, birch, rowan, Scots pine, holly, hazel, alder, willows, aspen, ash, wych elm, juniper, yew are all natives. Such obvious trees as larch and sycamore are incomers.

The road down to Kirkmichael (descending from Glen Derby).

The path comes out onto a dirt road. Turn right, for 300 m, then, signposted, left up a footpath past a bench. When the path forks keep right, which leads straight up to the lip of the gorge where the Black Spout is suddenly revealed. Two benches indicate its popularity with locals and visitors alike. An interpretative board is planned. There is a small fall, a short spate, and then a long plunge to the foot of a considerable amphitheatre. Some thinning of the trees would improve the view of the falls.

One short cut can be made from the falls. Descend by the gorge till the path swings right, back to the bench above the dirt track. Turn left onto this track and follow it down (golf course on right), passing under the railway, to come out on the old A9 south of Pitlochry. Where we turned off originally onto Knockfarrie Road the main road turns under the railway, passes Bell's Blair Atholl distillery (open to the public) and is joined by this track from the Black Spout. The old A9 then makes a short riverside sweep before traffic is fed up onto the new A9. The old road turns left (various signs for East Haugh, Dalshian, Croftinloan, pottery) to go under the railway again and runs on parallel with its new counterpart. We will rejoin it here shortly. Meanwhile, back to the Black Spout on the Edradour Burn.

Walk up the west bank of the Edradour gorge. There are many variant paths and, twice, cuttings push one in from the gorge but if a return is made to the edge of the gorge the continuation is clear. The wood ends at a wall with fields beyond. A signposted path goes off, top left, to Pitlochry; we bear off, top right, where there is a brief but bonny view up to Ben Vrackie. Don't take the path on by the edge of the field but the one angling down into the gorge, which soon leads to a footbridge, then wends up to a gate leading into a field. Follow up the right edge of the field to a kissing gate onto a farm track which leads into the farm Coilavoulin, and exit by its drive to Edradour. Coilavoulin is _wood of the mill_ and opposite the car park there was a mill building, which was already derelict early this century and has now disappeared. Milton of Edradour is another name indicating there being a mill at one time.

The buildings to the right are all part of the distillery, founded in 1825 by local farmers — and which you can visit (Easter–October, 0796 2095). The process is fascinating and one can only marvel at the ingenuity of our distant ancestors who invented distilling, while enjoying the wee sample that comes at the end of the tour.

Fortified, we turn down the small tarred road into the magnificent Tummel valley. Here, as with the view downwards from above Kinlochleven, we are given the finest of views from the _middle heights_: behind is Ben Vrackie, jagged, barren, brown (the world of the mountain), below is the Tummel, lush and quilted, green (the world of the valley). Relish the walk down rather than grudging the 100 m 'lost'. The road descends by Donavourd (a home) and Croftinloan (a school) to come out on the old A9. Turn left. Dalshian is passed (right) then, left, are some gates and a gatehouse. Immediately behind the house is a small road signposted Ballyoukan, then there is a bridge and telephone kiosk. The Ballyoukan road is the start of our route over the moors to Kirkmichael. Before tackling this steep ascent a five-minute walk further along the old A9 will bring one to the Pitlochry Pottery and Tea Room (Easter–October; 0796 82438), a pleasant indulgence coming at just the right time and place. Return to the Ballyoukan turn off once suitably refreshed.

In about 1 km this road rises from less than 100 m to 280 m. You will need bottom gear. The views open out quickly as a result of the steep climb. The tarred road gradually turns into a farm road, becoming unsurfaced from the bend right along a plantation at the upper cultivation level. The open moors lie beyond but much of the moorland has now been planted — to the destruction of some pleasant old paths. At present the forest gate is locked and there is no stile. Once over there is a track branching right and it is worth diverting down this for two minutes to an old sheepfank which gives a grand view down the great Tay valley. Return and carry on along the switchback main track, pleasant now but in a decade it will become a tunnel of conifers. The road passes west of Faire Mhor with its telecommunications mast on top. Keep to the lower of the two roads shown. There are good — last — views down to Pitlochry as Faire Mhor is passed. Loch Broom appears and, ahead, the road runs on to two huts (which will no doubt vanish as the trees grow taller). A track cutting down right, and another left (with notices saying Cairn Elrig and Creag Breac) should be ignored. Continue almost to the huts and then turn down to Loch Broom. The road ends at a boathouse at the north end of the loch.

Loch Broom actually drains to the River Tummel while, psychologically, it is at the head of Glen Derby. The watershed is a very innocuous one. The first mention of the loch comes with a Pictish battle being fought there in 729. Loch Broom is Loch *Bhraoin* (*loch of showers*). Glen Derby was originally Glen Dionaite (the *sheltered glen*) but in the early 18th century the owner Lord Nairne called it after his in-laws, the Earls of Derby.

As yet there is no stile to help one from Loch Broom to Glen Derby and the going is rough and untracked but a route can be teased out. Note the Allt Bunbruach, flowing into Loch Broom, has a split 1 km up, the other stream from this bifurcation flowing down as the Black Burn into Glen Derby. The road on past the huts can lead to the forest fence too but the slopes are purgatorially-deep heather and descending to Loch Broom is easier.

Descending Glen Derby aim for the Mains of Glenderby, both to pick up a track thereafter and for some interesting ruins in the vicinity. The Mains is an old shepherd's house with a large, walled sheepfank behind. It was only abandoned in the 1950s, but a fire ten years later gutted the building. The nettle patch indicates the house's rubbish dump and, down by the burn there is still a struggling clump of rhubarb. When there one July we saw a family of five kestrels hunting over the old run-rig patterns on the braes opposite.

Even more interesting is an old village 300 m up the burn. Several groups of houses exist, broad, long houses, facing the south with barns always at right-angles and several grain kilns still visible, one being in near-perfect condition. A reedy hollow may have been the old flax pool. Maps of the 18th century show many such villages in what was south Atholl land. This was Tomnafaul. With urban mills at Blairgowrie, and Perth and Dundee not too distant, it was a drift to the towns rather than vicious clearances that led to the abandoment of such settlements.

A rough track is picked up at the Mains and wends through a plantation before coming to the slopes down into Strath Ardle. The landscape has a certain Scandinavian look about it, which is reinforced by the scattered log-houses among the self-seeded trees, for these all have the turf roofs one sees across the North Sea. Names of places in Norway, Ireland and England reflect the illogical British habit of living in one place and naming one's house after somewhere else. An unlikely spread of sea buckthorn has established itself by the track. The Log Cabin Hotel is the real welcome to Kirkmichael which snuggles in the valley below, a rich landscape which contrasts with the sweep of empty Glen Derby.

The hamlet west of the river is really Williamstown. This plurality of names being very much a Highland habit, going back to the days when rivers divided rather than linked. We've already met it trans-Leven and trans-Tilt. The church, founded back in 1184, was largely rebuilt in 1792. Before then Kirkmichael did not exist. A bridge over the river collapsed in 1750 and thereafter people crossed on wooden planks. The Telford road from Pitlochry to Blairgowrie (now the A924) dates only to 1830, when the bridge was also rebuilt.

Kirkmichael is a tiny, tidy, Legoland village squeezed in on either side of the bridge. The school has two storeys as it could not expand horizontally and the church lies tightly wedged between road, bridge and river. There are a couple of shops and a coffee house. At the south end of the town is a big Celtic cross, a memorial to the local JP who died in 1900, 'erected by 350 of his friends who loved and trusted him'.

Accommodation: Kirkmichael

For its size Kirkmichael has a superabundance of overnight possibilities but some of it is rather *après ski* or up-market in atmosphere and price.

Hotels

Strathlene Hotel, Kirkmichael, PH10 7NT.   0250 81 347

Kirkmichael Hotel, Kirkmichael, PH10 7NT.   0250 81 386

Aldchlappie Hotel, Kirkmichael, PH10 7NS. (South end.) 0250 81 224

Log Cabin Hotel, Glen Derby, Kirkmichael, PH10 7NB. (Good food, but a bit out of the village.)   0250 81 228

B&B

Mrs J. Finch, Conachan, Kirkmichael, Blairgowrie, Perthshire. (North of the village.)   0250 81 226

Mr and Mrs Mills, Ardlebrig, Kirkmichael, Blairgowrie, Perthshire, PH10 7NY. (West over bridge.)   0250 81 350

Redhu House, Kirkmichael, Blairgowrie. (West over bridge.) 0250 81 302

Shops Early closing day is Wednesday.

Camping No site. Ask locally: the joiner owns the Banner Field across the bridge.

Reading Reid, A. G.: *Strathardle, Its History and Its People*, Blairgowrie, 1986.

Kerr, J.: *Old Roads to Strathardle*, Blair Atholl, 1984.

Alternative route

OS43

A. Blair Atholl to Spittal of Glen Shee (and thereafter to Glen Isla)

Strong hill walkers may like to keep to the hills a bit more once across the A9 and they could make a route from Blair Atholl to the Spittal of Glen Shee to Glen Isla instead of Blair Atholl to Kirkmichael to Glen Isla. There is also a pleasant crossing from Kirkmichael to the Spittal of Glen Shee. These routes are briefly described.

As far as Daldhu in Glen Fearnach the route is as described under Day 10A, Blair Atholl to Kirkmichael so is not repeated here (see p 133). Daldhu stands at a junction and one turns up the Glenn Fearnach track to cross the Allt Fearnach by a bridge. This estate track continues to Fealar Lodge which, standing at 570 m in big hills and being 18 km from a surfaced road, must be one of the remotest inhabited houses in the country. Walk up the road for ten minutes and then turn up the hillside to gain the Creag Dhubh ridge above its minor crags. I've twice met huge herds of red deer here. A col at 730 m (038727) leads to steeper, but easy, slopes down into tight Glen Lochsie.

Glen Lochsie Lodge is now a ruin. A new bulldozed track extends the one shown south of the burn right to the lodge and up the spur of Breacreidh above it. The railway from Hotel to Lodge has long been dismantled but its line can be traced on the ground. Most of the bridges shown in the glen are in parlous state, or have disappeared, so one side or other of the glen has to be chosen at the lodge. The old railway route down to the Dalmunzie Hotel is less arduous, and the hotel offers half the accommodation opportunities of the area. Dalmunzie (*the mossy meadow*) appears in 16th-century sources and an older castle across the river was a MacIntosh stronghold. The present castellated building went up in 1880. The 2 km drive down to the Spittal has many different trees along it. This day's route is best avoided in the stalking season, as is the continuation to Glen Isla.

B. Kirkmichael to Spittal of Glen Shee (13 km; 320 m)

Retrace the $2\frac{1}{2}$ km of paths up the west side of Strath Ardle — the end of the route yesterday — and cross back to Enochdhu, on the A924. The right-of-way to the Spittal of Glen Shee is signposted.

The 'Giant's Grave' beside the house drive is a Pictish burial mound. Supposedly Prince Ardle routed the Danes at Enochdhu (*black meadow*) but the fleeing Vikings turned and killed Ardle and two followers who had over-enthusiastically pursued the invaders. This is their grave, marked by a tall stone at the head and a boulder at the foot: $5\frac{1}{2}$ m apart.

Go up the estate track past several houses and through a farmyard. After about 2 km the track forks. Take the left fork, which crosses the Allt Dubhagan, and skirts on under the conical hill, Elrig, to the upper reaches of the Allt Doire nan Eun. A path crosses this burn and climbs steeply to the 650 m pass, An Lairig, where the Glen Shee scenery is suddenly open to view. A steep, grassy 2 km descent takes one down to the Spittal of Glen Shee. This old right-of-way is shown on Roy's map of 1755. Queen Victoria rode over the pass in 1844, had a night at Kindrogan and went on via Glen Derby to Dunkeld. In 1866 she came over the pass, this time going to Pitlochry, a visit which gave that town quite a boost.

The Spittal of Glen Shee, under its guardian hill, Ben Gulabin, is the last spread of green valley on the famous road over the Cairnwell Pass to Deeside. 'Spittal' bears the old meaning of hospital or hospice and drovers, packmen, reivers and travellers of all sorts must have stayed here over the centuries. The antiquity of the site is emphasized by a standing stone on a knoll behind the church. This building dates only to 1822, before that it was a crude 'chapel of ease', the meeting place for locals who could not make the parish church which was at Kirkmichael. There are some weird tombstones in the graveyard and I noticed one memorial stone to someone killed on the Matterhorn. There is a magnificent old hump-backed bridge which, until a decade ago, bore all the heavy modern traffic. Now cars tend to zoom past the Spittal at twice the speed of seeing anything. We pedestrians have the best of it. 'Shee' comes from the Gaelic for 'fairy' and the glen is particularly rich in Celtic lore, most memorably the story of the fatal boar hunt of Diarmid. The story is equally vigorously claimed for Kintail and Argyll and other places, so is obviously one that made a deep impression. Wells and hills with the name boar (_tuirc_) are common — as boars once were — and several have conscripted this old Irish story:

Diarmid had been beguiled by Fingal's wife Grainne and carried her off on her wedding night. Fingal pretended friendship and arranged a hunt against a great boar which had a poisonous spine in its hide, his hope being that Diarmid would receive a fatal wound. The young hero instead slew the boar. Fingal then asked him to measure it and when he came back from doing so asked him to do so again from tail to snout to verify its great size. This time, in doing so, Diarmid's heel caught against the fatal spine. As he lay dying he begged Fingal to fetch water from a nearby well. Eventually, overcome by remorse, he fetched water, but it was too late ...

┌─Accommodation: Spittal of Glen Shee─┐

Dalmunzie Hotel, Glenshee, PH10 7LJ. 025 085 224
Spittal of Glenshee Hotel, Glenshee PH10 7QF. 025 085 215
Mrs Mackay, Dalhenzean, Glenshee, PH10 7QD. 025 085 217 (pre-booking essential)

This is a fairly short stage and it would be possible to push on to upper Glenisla the same day. Dalvanie 187659 offers farmhouse accommodation in a superb setting and is highly recommended. There are even deer at the bottom of the garden.

Mrs Campbell, Dalvanie Farmhouse, Folda, Glenisla, Perthshire, PH11 8QW.   057 582 316.

Camping Wild camping is rather restricted but ask at a farm.

Reading Miller, T. D.: *Tales of a Highland Parish (Glenshee)*, Perth, 1929.

C. Glen Shee to Glen Isla

Leave the Spittal of Glenshee at a farm on the A93 and follow the track to ill-sounding Tomb, then on to Westerton of Runavey where a track leads up onto the moors. There are several tracks bearing off but keep to the one which pulls up into Gleann Carnach where it peters out. Head for the col between Black Hill and Monamenach. The latter is a Corbett and a very easy ascent from the col. A fence leads up to the summit and one possibility is to continue south then descend eastwards by a stalkers' path to Auchavan.

A low-level option is to cut through by Loch and Glen Beanie, south of the Monamenach hills, down to Dalvanie. From the Black Hill—Monamenach col a steep descent leads to Tulchan Lodge at the head of Glen Isla. A famous old drovers' route from Deeside comes over Glas Maol and off ,Monega Hill to Glen Isla nearby. The head of Glen Isla has some spectacular corries, famous for their rich flora. Follow the estate road down the glen and cross to the east bank of the Isla just before Auchavan. The 5 km of walking down to Little Forter is singularly attractive. On one spring coast-to-coast we were impressed by the abundance of lamb twins and triplets, the first we'd seen on the crossing and indicative that we'd made the rich glens of Angus. Either side of the Isla valley can be followed from Little Forter to Brewlands Bridge whence 3 km of B951 lead to Kirkton of Glenisla. (Described on p 179.)

D. Kirkmichael to Alyth (saving a day)
OS53

This alternative could take a day off the crossing but gives walking entirely on tarred roads and misses out some interesting country, so is only briefly described. Leave Kirkmichael by the A924 down Strath Ardle but bear left almost at once to follow the B950 eastwards to Glenshee, $5\frac{1}{2}$ km, where one turns right onto the A93, mercifully for only $1\frac{1}{2}$ km, as traffic is apt to be travelling fast and is none too careful about pedestrians. Just $\frac{1}{2}$ km north from the junction with the A93 is the Dalrulzion Hotel while $\frac{1}{2}$ km south is a farm coffee-cum-craft shop and $\frac{1}{2}$ km on again is the Blackwater Inn. Just 300 m beyond the Blackwater Inn turn left on the minor road for Alyth.

The road pulls up from the Black Water bridge and gives some fine views, to Highlands and Lowlands then after 7 or 8 km the uplands are left and the richer lands of Angus begin. The Banff Estate occupies much of the land left of the road down.

When the road joins the one circuiting the Hill of Alyth turn right to follow down the Den of Alyth. A _den_ is an eastern Scots word for a steep, wooded glen and this one, with trees descended from the original forests of Scotland, is most attractive. At 225493 leave the road and take to the riverside path(s) which go down into Alyth. The forest is mostly oak, ash, hazel, wych-elm and much loved by red squirrels. At Alyth we rejoin the main route, described on p 186.

Glen Isla

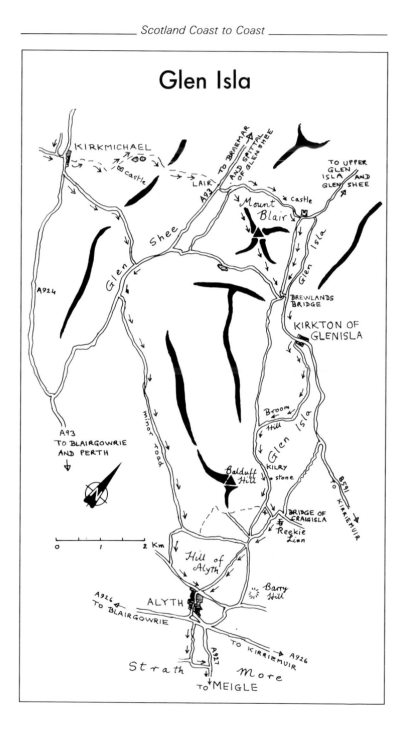

Day 11

By Mount Blair to Glen Isla

OS43, 44

The first part of this day is described in greater detail than most as it goes across cultivated land as a right-of-way which is not too clearly signposted in places. A general 'follow the stream for seven kilometres' may be enough in Lochaber, but here wayfinding needs a field-by-field outline. Guide posts are often not visible when wanted and the path often unclear. The walking is very pleasant and one companion on a recent walk called it 'the day of the curlews'.

The route leaves Kirkmichael from next the Strathlene/Kirkmichael Hotels and is clearly signposted. It begins as an oddly English-style sunken lane ('sunk into the wet' was suggested) which twists up through several fields, with several gates/stiles. Keep up the left of the (last) field with its shelter belt of trees to a bigger stile over a wall onto rougher pastures. There are three clumps of trees on the skyline; aim to pass just left of the right, less densely planted, group of trees. A few posts with arrows may be met on the route but they are unusually close to the stiles rather than in the open. Keep on beyond the trees and down to the corner of the plantation that backs this clump of trees to a gate/stile over a wall. The route so far is clear enough on the map but the continuation is misleading and should not be followed.

Do not bear right to a bridge visible in the valley bottom. This would bring you up to Achintully Castle, a 16th-century tower, now the local big house, which is well hidden in trees but, in line with two marker posts, aim slightly left across the

'Ready for the road': setting out from the Strathlene Hotel in Kirkmichael.

The lochans above Achintully on the Kirkmichael-Lair route.

field to a gate that can be seen in the fence (no stile). Through the gate, descend more or less directly to the stream (the Allt Menach) where there is a footbridge and right-of-way signs. The bridge is not visible from the gate or further back which is why people go astray earlier. From here on every wall has a stile and there are often posts beside them, so these will not be mentioned each time.

From the stream the route heads up to the end of a shelter belt of trees (the more southerly of the two shown on the map) and along through it on the same line. Cross another field and, leaving the castle grounds on the right, a farm road is reached (on map) and crossed to reach fields beyond. (Wild raspberries grow by the stile here.) Keep up by the wall on the right of this, and the next, with a plantation to the east. The farm road indicated on the map does not really show on the ground till, at the top of the second field, the open moorland is reached and the farm track becomes very clear.

Achintully Castle was the seat of the notorious Spalding family who seemed to be at perpetual feud with everyone. They gained their original foothold in Angus as a reward for helping Robert the Bruce. Only 1 km to the NW stands the ruins of Whitefield Castle build by Malcolm Canmore as a hunting lodge (he also built one in Braemar) for lower Strath Ardle in those days was a thorny wilderness much loved by wild boar.

Follow the track which rises and swing right to pass above two lochans (the first, much overgrown, has a noisy, black-headed gull nesting site). After a gate the track forks. Take the right fork (post) which runs along a line of butts before twisting down into the valley of Coire a' Bhaile. (The clump of trees shown on the map has gone.)

Leave the road at the foot of the descent, left, to cross a footbridge to reach a stile over a wall. The path (often just a linking of odd sheep tracks) traverses up the heathery slopes ahead to pass over the saddle of a small spur, following the line shown rather optimistically on the map. There are some marker posts but these are often not inter-visible. There are several ruins in the heather indicating more prosperous times.

In misty weather care is needed to go through the col and

Mount Blair above Glen Shee — from the road near Lair.

down to Lair. The route is not obvious even in good conditions. Traverse along odd sheep tracks to the col, where a solitary larch on the Lamh Dearg slopes is a useful landmark, and take its right, eastern, slopes where there are odd posts leading along to a stile over a wall at the far end. Head NE from the stile to descend to and then follow the Allt an Lair's south bank, keeping along above its deeply cut course. Mount Blair only comes into view as the col is left so take the chance of studying its ascent line. The hill is often dark, being heathery, and its symmetrical shape is very easy to spot from many directions, so it is odd how invisible it has been on today's approach.

The A93 is joined briefly at Lair but before turning off onto the B951 note the little granite cross just up from the junction, on the east side of the road. In 1906 a beautiful American girl was thrown from a coach here when the horses bolted. She died in a nearby house and the locals erected a concrete cross in her memory. After the last war an old American visited the glen — her brother. By then the memorial was crumbling so he arranged for the present cross to be made. The memorial stands in a tiny garden, noticed by few of the motorists hurrying down the Lair brae. The horses pulling Queen Victoria's coach also bolted on one occasion and were only just halted before the brae. At the top of the brae is an interesting pottery: a good change to see craftsmen at work — without the temptation of buying something!

The B951 wends down and along to cross the Shee Water then, shortly after, one is presented with a choice of routes. The best is simply to go over Mount Blair (see below), a fine wee hill in its own right, or to circuit it either to the north or to the south. North about, the B951, is marginally easier. Once Glen Isla is reached by this route one could turn off to pass Forter and Little Forter, then walk down the minor road on the east of Glen Isla, or the A951 could simply be followed down to Brewlands Bridge.

Forter Castle was built in 1560 and was burnt in 1640 at the same time as the Earl of Airlie's main house, down where the Isla reaches the Strathmore farmlands. The Covenanting Earl of Argyll was behind this attack and later, in revenge, Montrose burnt Argyll's Castle Campbell in the Ochils. Castles go but songs remain: *The Bonnie Hoose o' Airlie* and *The Campbells are Coming* from that unpleasant story.

South about Mount Blair has more variety. Blacklunans sees one turn east again. Drumore, alas, is no longer a hotel. The Drumore Loch has a fish farm, which attracts the local ospreys! This road also leads down to Brewlands Bridge. Brewlands was originally called Pentecost and was one of several brewhouses in Glenisla (the village is spelt as one word) mentioned in the 16th century. Alas there is not even a pub now. A modern bridge has replaced the older bridge; cross either and turn right, south for the 2 km remaining to Kirkton of Glenisla: a small scattered hamlet, set in beautiful surroundings, as picnic areas and car parks suggest.

Mount Blair is a hill many walkers see from many other summits but cannot name or even place accurately. The summit of this dark, heather hill, bump heaped on bump in remarkable symmetry, commands a huge panorama of Highlands and Lowlands. The ascent is straighforward and a North–South traverse works into our scheme admirably.

Once across the Shee Water turn left, north, and shortly one comes to Cray, just a church building and manse, which now serve secular rather than religious functions. Cray is

Left *Glenisla — the rich lands between Brewlands Bridge and the Kirkton.*

Below left *Kirkton of Glenisla: the restful garden of the Kirkside House Hotel.*

Right *One of two old cheese presses at the Dalmunzie Hotel at Glen Shee.*

Below *The Spittal of Glen Shee — the old church and the military road bridge nestle below Ben Gulabin.*

supposed to come from *Caraidh*. At Drumnaskelloch on the southern slopes of Mount Blair the Picts and Scots are said to have fought a battle. Tobar-na-caen (*well of the heads*) marks the spot. The Scots were in flight round the hill when a local man rushed out with a scythe screaming 'Caraidh! Caraidh!' (*Turn! Turn!*) and so swung the battle that the Picts were defeated.

At the bend just beyond Cray go through a gate onto the open hillside and make a rising traverse towards the strip of trees on the hill's NW ridge. Follow up beside the trees (the highest trees are mostly dead, from being planted too high) and then on alongside a fence which leads all the way to the summit cairn/trig point, 744 m. There is a grand view along Glen Shee from this route up. The ornate castle, Dalnaglar, in the foreground was built in 1864, in best Balmoral baronial, the work of Gilbert Scott. The name means *field of the ford* and was once the crossing for travellers heading north from Glen Isla.

Mount Blair is no worse for being neither Munro nor Corbett but then, from Tinto to Ben Stack, there are plenty of meritorious summits below those artificial, antique heights. Roe deer may be seen on the ascent and mountain hares most certainly will — a pleasing sign of being in the east. The varied wildlife has left a useful trod up both sides of the fence, the northern being easier as it is less cluttered with discarded fence posts.

The summit cairn has a grave under it, of one Alex Robertson, who hanged himself from a beam placed across a lime kiln (the ruin of which stands by the Blackwater). In the good old days suicides were denied burial in consecrated grounds and often a spot at the meeting of parishes or properties would be chosen to bury the unfortunate. Some Glenisla men thought the top of Mount Blair sounded rather improbable so they dug up the ground early last century — and duly found the bones of a man.

A more man-trodden path runs along the fence down the SE Ridge, which can then be abandoned almost anywhere to descend to the Blacklunans–Brewlands Bridge road. There are small crags to avoid and one should study the route from above. The col before Over Craig (called Geack of the Barnetts) is one easy line and leads down to the path shown which gives easy access to the road.

I've also descended well down the east ridge, in search of the Tobar-na-Caen (or Tobar a' Chinn as it is on the 1:100,000) but did not discover the well.

Corrie Vanoch, between the NE and E ridges, once held a famous well (spring) which had curative powers, particularly for children, who were carried up for a ceremony at dawn on the first Sunday in May. In these more sceptical days such wells seem to have lost their efficacy! Mount Blair's lower slopes are covered with the sites of hut circles and prehistoric cairns. The area probably had a larger population 4,000 years ago than it does today. The NE Ridge and down Corrie Vanoch is another easy route off the hill.

One walks off sheet 43 between Brewlands Bridge and Kirkton of Glenisla and as there are only three grid squares involved on this and the early part of tomorrow's route one could simply make some notes from the bottom corner of sheet 44 rather than carry the whole map. The rest of tomorrow is on sheet 53. Note the bridge opposite the school before the Kirkton is reached. It is crossed on the morrow. Kirkton is *church town*, Glenisla as the name implies is an area rather than a village. Often a village would spring up round the site chosen for the kirk. Kirkton is a very common name.

Manse and church date back to the early 19th century and the then incumbent was a fiery Mr Burns, who could hold his drink with the best. Smuggling was at its zenith at the time and the families of those so engaged could suffer severely if culprits were caught but community-conscious clergymen were often on the side of the poor locals. Any excise party riding into Glenisla would pause at the hotel, which did not go unobserved from the nearby manse windows. The minister would lead out his horse as if taking it out to graze but, out of sight, he was up and off. Obtaining saddle and bridle at the first opportunity he would gallop through the glen waving his hat and yelling 'The Philistines be upon thee, Samson', which must have been an extraordinary spectacle. But it was also a code and in his wake figures would head for the hills with their precious copper 'heads and worms'. Mr Burns had a nature described as somewhat choleric and a tale remains of a baptism when, things not going smoothly, he seized the water vessel being brought to fill the font, and poured the entire contents over the infant's head!

Tidings of a raid were once received by a household in upper Glenisla when they had a large amount of barley fermenting in their barn; it was too much to hide and too late to remove it. Someone then had a brainwave. A field lay ploughed, ready for sowing, so the incriminating grain was sacked, thrown on a cart, and taken to the field where the sacks were in the process of being dropped off at regular intervals when the excise party passed — and gave the hard-working farm folk their wishes for a good sowing and future harvest.

The copper 'worm' was an expensive item and its loss was serious. Seeing the excise approaching one of two brothers shoved some kitchen utensils in a sack and tore off up the hill behind the house. The excisemen leapt from their horses in pursuit and after being led a merry dance caught up on the fugitive who then declared there was no law against a man running about with a sack of his belongings. Meanwhile his brother had quietly walked down the road with the vital evidence.

One entry in the kirk session records was unusual: 'May 5, 1745. It being reported that Mr Anderson, in slavery on the coast of Barbary, for whose ransom a collection has been made, was now liberated, the £3 Scots collected to be restored'.

Accommodation: Kirkton of Glenisla

Kirkside House Hotel, Kirkton of Glenisla, by Blairgowrie, PH11 8PH. 057 582 278

Glenisla Hotel, Kirkton of Glenisla, by Blairgowrie. 057 582 223

Highland Adventure Activity Centre, Knockshannoch, Glenisla, Perthshire, PH11 8PE. 057 582 207/238

As one walks into the hamlet the Kirkside House Hotel (Mr and Mrs Davidson) is on the right and the Glenisla Hotel on the left. I've used the former several times and have enjoyed my visits. The hotel has a fine garden setting above the river and the reception is friendly and helpful.

Camping Wild camping from now on becomes difficult as we are into well-used farmland, with few suitable untended corners. Ask at the Kirkside Hotel.

The Glenisla Hotel offers pony trekking if one would like a day off to bruise new areas of one's anatomy. The Activity Centre offers many outdoor sports facilities as well and also does B&B. It is situated 2 km further down the glen on the B951 Kirriemuir road (on sheet 53).

Reading Grewar, D.: _The Story of Glenisla_, Aberdeen, 1926.

Smith, W. McCombie: _The Romance of Poaching in the Highlands_, 1904 (reprinted 1984).

Meigle–Glamis

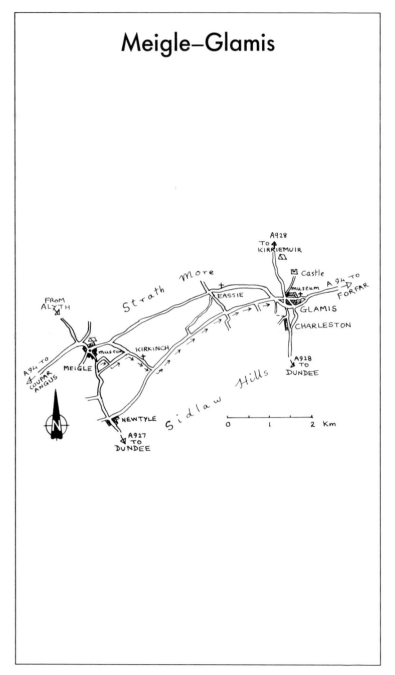

Day 12

Out of the hills to Alyth and Meigle

OS53 (44)

The character of the walk changes again as we descend the Braes of Angus into ever-richer farmland. This is really the last day with a mountainy feeling so we make the most of it; with the tarred roads ahead the last kindly paths and tracks are used as much as possible. The quality of landscape alters. It does not diminish. I would go so far as to say the Braes of Angus have a quality of richness which the wet deserts of big hills rather lack. Today we rediscover 'how green greens can be, and the glory of the tree'. Gaelic names give way to Scots names too.

Our day begins with a short walk back up the road to the footbridge below the school but if an early morning paddle appeals then the ford just below the Kirkside Hotel could be used to 'save' some circuiting. The ford is the start of the old road to Alyth so has a certain historic lure. Those who prefer dry feet can 'aye gang roon'. Once across the footbridge go up a side burn to the larger track and turn left along this to a gate into a field. The track follows the right edge of this field to a gate into the road up from the ford. The monument above the River Isla is to a Victorian landowner, erected by his friends 'who knew his worth'.

The road can hardly be lost as it simply follows down the valley of the River Isla but some care is still needed as most of the farms display no names and there have been several new plantings and roads which are not shown on the First Series Map. The Second Series Map is a worthwhile investment.

Dykehead (Kilry) Church in Glenisla.

One's whereabouts can be gauged by looking at features across the valley: the B951 snakes off through behind Craiglee Hill. Less visible is Knockshannoch, a *round-shaped* mansion house which was for many years a youth hostel and is now the Highland Activity Centre.

There are several tracks which traverse up from the old road but these should all be ignored. Frequently they run into new plantings, not on any map yet, or lead to dead-ends. Scruschloch Farm is the last before the old road makes its swing upwards, about 300 m on from this unpronounceable farm name (junction: 229569). The road shown going on ahead to Loanhead is a new farm track and though possible, it is not the old right-of-way and misses out some good scenery. Keep to the old way, passing a house (with a superb view) to a gate, from which an unsurfaced road skirts Brook Hill, runs along a shelter belt of trees and comes out into the hill road from Brewlands Bridge (223563). Looking up this road Mount Blair rises in friendly familiarity beyond the top of the pass. This area teams with rabbits, as does most of the country for the rest of today. The road descends steeply to Little Kilry then turns along the valley bottom following the Burn of Kilry. There is a house with an attractive garden on the left, and behind it, in the wood near the river, is a big standing stone. An attempt last century failed to shift the monolith. The local school is passed, right, and after $\frac{1}{2}$ km the road divides at Kilry Parish Church. The right fork leads more directly to Alyth but we take the left fork to visit what many consider the finest waterfall of the walk.

Have a look inside the churchyard first: the church stands, not among tombstones but in a trim garden. With the church, the old manse and other buildings all painted white and picked out in the local red sandstone, there is a sudden feeling of rural England, or Scottish Lowlands at least. The manse is now a private house as the minister lives at Lintrathen, having the joint charge of Kilry, Lintrathen and Glenisla.

Taking the left fork a ruler-straight road runs down to the B954. Turn left along to Bridge of Craigisla. There is a small rural store on the left and on the right the walled policies of Craigisla House. A sign points to the Reekie Linn but the north side of the river offers better prospects so cross the Craigisla Bridge (an important one historically as you could imagine) and then turn right through a car park to gain the woodland path beyond. There are several good viewing points and you can also go down to the rocks on the lip of the falls — an interesting place when the river is in spate; then the two-tiered plunge becomes a single, awesome turmoil of yellow power. The pool at the foot is 30 m deep. A cave, the Black Dub, was the site of a local laird's hiding place after he'd killed a man. Nightly invitations by the devil in the guise of a black dog however made him decide to surrender to the law. *Reek* is a lowland Scots word for smoke, hence *Auld Reekie* for Edinburgh, and *Reekie Linn* for this 'smoke that thunders'. Sarah Murray, a pioneer guidebook writer, waxed enthusiastic about this fall and Stott reckons it 'the finest fall of its kind in the East of Scotland'.

After visiting the falls return to the bridge over the Isla and take the B954 south for 2 km. As the road begins to rise there is a milestone showing 'Alyth $3\frac{1}{2}$'. The road beyond bends sharply to the left and a smaller road breaks off right, signposted to Banff. In the angle of this junction a farm track is signposted 'Hill of Loyal Walk to Alyth' and is our route, the last touch of unsurfaced track for the crossing. The 'Hill of Alyth' sign should be ignored.

Anyone fanatical about prehistoric hill forts could stay on

the B954 in order to visit Barry Hill. There is a gate just south of the top of the pass between Barry Hill and Hill of Loyal which gives access to the site. (In late May the hill is a mass of yellow mountain pansies.) The summit is hollow and there are big ditches and dykes, all much more visible than is normal with hilltop forts. Continue on the B954/B952 in to Alyth. This road alternative is rather dangerous so is only recommended for brave antiquarians. The old road over between Hill of Loyal and Hill of Alyth is the right, worthy end to the rough walking.

The route is lined all the way by oak trees (youngsters of 100+ years), there is some birch at the start and a double line of sycamores in the middle where the green road is a bit sunken and wet and has a rash of young willows. There is also a line of single wooden poles carrying a power cable. All the gates have wicket gates beside them for pedestrians. The Hill of Loyal wood is oak, with some larch to the north, and the Hill of Alyth is chrome-coloured for weeks on end by the acres of gorse. Follow the path right through the pass before making the (optional but recommended) ascent to the Hill of Alyth trig point, 295 m. There is a sign indicating 'Alyth Hill View Point' etc and a gate leading onto a bigger farm road which leads down to Alyth. It becomes tarred and a side branch goes off to the Lands of Loyal Hotel. All the various routes over or round the Hill of Alyth merge at the top of the

Descending to Alyth, the striped field is due to rows of raspberry plants.

town where there are some attractive old houses. The three crumbling arches are all that remain of the medieval church of St Moluag.

The steep Toutie Street leads down into the town. This odd name recalls the noise of the herd boys' horns as they took their cattle up to graze on Alyth Hill. On the left we pass the Losset Inn and the Old Stables B&B (entrance through the builders' yard) to then run alongside the Alyth Burn (Commercial Street). A small, local history Folk Museum is passed (open: May–Sept, Tues–Sat, 1–5 pm), also the Alyth Hotel. Crossing to the Square and then left, leads down the town's main street (Airlie Street) — with possibly the first bank available since Fort William! The Singing Kettle offers a wide range of refreshments and food to weary walkers and, across the road, Walkers Bakery has a range of home-made biscuits. Alyth is all the more delightful for not being on any Tourist Trail. It is a pleasant wee market town. There is a lively annual Agricultural Show held at the end of June. Meigle, where we end the day's walking, has limited accommodation so if a bed is not available simply phone for a taxi and return to Alyth for the night.

The country changes again after Alyth. The hill country for us is really finished; the Sidlaw Hills, behind Dundee, which we see to the SE, are Lowland Hills. The Highland Line runs through Alyth. The huge valley below is the rich farmland country of Strathmore, which we walk across to reach Meigle.

Leaving Alyth take the *right* fork at the war memorial, turn left at the A926 and then right again almost at once to go down a quiet, safe, farm road past Newton of Bathary to Netherton and so round to the B954. This can be a busy road and a rather frightening re-introduction to the world of noise, speed and fumes. The Bridge of Crathies is our farewell to the River Isla, now a meandering river which loops on through Strathmore, adding the waters of Glen Shee and Strath Ardle before entering the Tay near the unique Meikleour Beech Hedge. The short bit of A94 into Meigle is a reminder of really busy roads, being the main Perth–Aberdeen road. Meigle desperately needs a by-pass.

There are two main reasons for pushing on to Meigle, rather than just staying in Alyth; Meigle has a museum which

Alyth - a welcome to the Lowland scenery of the east.

simply must not be missed and Glamis has major attractions which are only open in the afternoon so our schedule is designed to take in all of these. There may not be any more hills but there is still plenty to explore.

If the museum is locked the key can be obtained from the custodian's house, which is the one with the plaques bearing arms diagonally opposite the Kinloch Arms Hotel. The custodian is an enthusiast and will gladly show anyone round and point out all the interesting features. An old hall is filled with the country's finest collection of Pictish symbol stones, those mysterious and exquisite carvings from the dawn of history. Many of the symbols are of natural animals, brilliantly executed. The 'fish' is obviously a salmon, not a trout or anything else and sea eagle and golden eagle are distinct. There are seahorses. And there are animals that are imaginary including a 'swimming elephant' — about which everyone will speculate. Then there are the numerous symbols of objects, like mirror and comb, and others which are purely abstract: crescents and V-rods, decorative lozenges and so on. These can appear on stones by

A 'trades' gravestone in the churchyard in Meigle.

One of the extraordinary Pictish symbol stones in Meigle Museum.

themselves or in any combination but other stones will have Christian symbols as well so whatever they stood for was not offensive to Christianity which often took over old stones and used the back for carving intricate crosses. Once discovered these stones became fascinating — so I'll leave your eyes (and ears) to enjoy their serendipity at Meigle.

Accommodation: Meigle, Alyth, etc

The Kinloch Arms stands in the centre of Meigle and if rather unpretentious to look at, there is a warm welcome within and excellent food. Being the local pub there is always good company in the evening. (The Saturday disco night might not appeal so much to weary walkers.) The Belmont Arms, 2 km on the Newtyle–Dundee road has just two rooms. The Kings of Kinloch is expensive and dinner formal — not really a hikers' hostelry! There is a bit of a shortage of beds for walkers in Meigle but a taxi can take one to/from Alyth for the night if need be.

Kinloch Arms Hotel, The Square, Meigle, Perthshire, PH12 3PT. 08284 251

Belmont Arms Hotel, Meigle, Perthshire, PH12 8J. 08284 232

Kings of Kinloch Hotel, Meigle, Perthshire, PH12 8QX. 08284 273

Meigle House Hotel, Meigle, Perthshire. 08284 270

Camping There is a small camping/caravan ground as one enters Meigle, but its future may not be certain.

Alyth

Alyth Hotel, 6 Commercial Street, Alyth, Perthshire. 08283 2447

Drumnacree House Hotel, St Ninian's Road, Alyth, Perthshire. 08283 2194

Lands of Loyal Hotel, Alyth, Perthshire, PH11 8QJ. (Mansion in garden; French cooking.) 08283 3151/2

The Losset Inn, Losset Road, Alyth, Perthshire, PH11 8BT. 08283 2393

The Old Stables, Losset Road, Alyth, Perthshire, PH11 8BT. 08283 2547

Yewbank, Banff Road, Alyth, Perthshire, PH11 8DR. 08283 2403

Ardler, (3 km SW of Meigle), Mrs Turner, The Old Manse. 08284 234

Blairgowrie, 6 km west of Alyth is a major tourist town with over thirty hotels and B&Bs listed. Tourist Office: 26 Wellmeadow, Blairgowrie, Perthshire, PH10 6AS (0250 2960), and **Couper Angus**, 4 km from Meigle has three hotels and several B&Bs. Details from the Blairgowrie Tourist Office.

Shops Meigle has a village shop; early closing day is Thursday. Alyth early closing day is Wednesday.

Taxis Meigle 407, Alyth 2672, Glamis 270, Blairgowrie 2116.

Day 13

Glamis day

OS53, 54

This is the shortest day's walking on the crossing but if the various visits are undertaken at Glamis legs can feel quite tired at the end of the day. In spring especially the walk gives a colourful panorama: from tree-lined roads over patchwork fields, splashed with yellow rape, to the range of the Mounth, blue-tinted hills, fringed with snow, a big cloudscape overhead. I don't think it is just reaction to what has gone before: Strathmore has superb scenery.

Walk out of Meigle on the B954 Newtyle–Dundee road, past the museum and school. Just beyond the last houses

---

The rich farmland in Strathmore on the walk from Miegle to Glamis.

Looking to Kinpurney Hill in the Sidlaws from Kirkinch church.

the road bends right (Belmont Castle grounds) and a small road turns off left at what was once a church. The road is signposted for 'Cottage Hospital' and when the trim hospital is reached swing right on what soon becomes a farm track. A fine garden is being made round the one house after the hospital. Turn left when the tarred road is met and then right at the next junction (just after the line of pylons is passed) to reach the pretty hamlet of Kirkinch. An old village, Kirkinch has been restored and poshed-up: a ponies and Range Rovers rural pad which looks like somewhere in the Home Counties rather than over the hills from Dundee. *Church-island* it may once have been: an old church sits up on a natural motte, a good viewpoint to the Sidlaws. The tower to the south, noticeable these last two days, is on Kinpurney Hill, another prehistoric fort site. There are several 17th-century slabs in or by the church and one tiny, heart-shaped stone, reading 'Dear Willie'.

Continue on to the Newtyle–Glamis road which runs along the base of the Sidlaws, no doubt the older road built there to run above the softness of the valley bottom, long before modern drainage and agriculture changed things and the A94 arrived. (A writer 100 years ago mentions the climate of Glamis being 'much healthier since the swamps and mosses have been drained'.) Turn left and just follow this road all the way to Glamis. There are magnificent sycamores along the road and the views, both up to the near hills and across Strathmore, are a changing kaleidoscope of colour: road-walking at its best. Eassie is a scattered hamlet otherwise there are just farms along the road. Eassie school had an oystercatcher on the roof once when I passed and the plain church is unusual in having all its windows of clear glass. Built in the early 19th century it replaced one whose roof had fallen in — a week after the minister had told his sabbath congregation to go off and take in the harvest. Many took this disaster as a judgement. If the museum at Meigle was enjoyed then the church by Eassie Farm on the A94 is worth a visit one day (when motoring) to see the fine symbol stone in the ruins. Our quiet road eventually comes down to the A94 which is crossed to reach Glamis beyond. The village is mercifully by-passed now.

Accommodation: Glamis (or Meigle/Alyth/Forfar)

Just where you go in Glamis depends on where you are staying. Accommodation is limited but, as with Meigle, a taxi can always take one off to Alyth or Forfar for the night. (Taxis: Glamis 270, Meigle 407, Forfar, 64855, 63760.) I have stayed in Charleston rather than Glamis as the friendly B&B on the crest of the hill has such a splendid situation. As soon as our quiet road meets the A94 turn up a farm road and into the woods to join a horizontal path leading to the north end of Charleston. When the tarred road up from Glamis is met, the house is just across the road: the only house on the east side, Charleston houses being in a row down the west of this road.

Mrs Scott, 'Lera', Charleston, Glamis, Angus. 030 784 508

At the lower end of Charleston, the Charleston Inn (030 784 266) has a deserved reputation for good meals.

Halfway between Glamis and Meigle is Castleton House, Glamis, Angus, DD8 1SJ, 030 784 340, which does country house B&B but not evening meals.

If going into Glamis itself cross the A94 as soon as it is reached and so into the village.

Mrs Collinson, 7 Main Street, Glamis, Angus. 030 784 200

Mrs Wilkie, 16 Main Street, Glamis, Angus. 030 784 419

These are the only regular B&Bs but the Manse (030 784 304) may well take in anyone really stuck for a bed. In the manse grounds is a huge symbol stone with a cross and symbols on one side, on the other bold symbols only, including a life-like salmon. Picasso could not have bettered the simple lines and effectiveness of these anonymous artists of the past.

Glamis has several shops and the Strathmore Arms is a renowned but reasonably priced restaurant which also offers accommodation.

Strathmore Arms, Main Street, Glamis, Angus, DD8 1RS. 030 784 248

The food is both plentiful and good, as various awards and recognitions suggest.

Forfar lies 7 km NE of Glamis along the busy A94 and, being a big market town, can offer a range of accommodation from the posh Royal Hotel to simple B&Bs. Next to the Municipal Buildings (Queen Street) is the Rupali Indian Restaurant which I'd recommend.

Forfar gives its name to Forfar bridies — a sort of super

pastie — well worth buying for the last picnic.

The tourist office address is: The Myre, Forfar. 0307 67876

Royal Hotel, Castle Street, Forfar. 0307 62691
The Stag Hotel, 142 Castle Street, Forfar. 0307 62737
Jarman's Hotel, 97 North Street, Forfar. 0307 64531
Queen's Hotel, The Cross, Forfar. 0307 62533
Plough Inn, 48 Market Street, Forfar 0307 62006

B&B

Mrs Craig, 20 Craog o' Loch Road, Forfar. 0307 67768
Mrs Gourley, 10 Manor Street, Forfar. 0307 64780
Mrs Irvine, 6 Westfield Drive, Forfar. 0307 62936
Mrs Tyrie, 35 Westfield Crescent, Forfar, DD8 1EG. 0307 62830
Mrs Webster, 17 Academy Street, Forfar, DD8 2HA. 0307 63099

There are several other B&Bs not listed, but equally good.

Above *The right end of the museum cottages — one can walk right through the whole long building.*

Left *The big symbol stone standing in the Manse garden at Glamis.*

One word of warning. The middle of July sees an annual Strathmore Vintage Extravaganza for which accommodation in Glamis is booked-up months in advance.

Shops Glamis has a village shop, early closing day Thursday. Forfar is 'county town' in scope.

Forfar bridies (called by J. M. Barrie 'a sublime kind of pie') can be traced back to a Margaret Bridie of Glamis, born in 1789 who made and sold her pasties at the local markets. Like to try the recipe when you return home?

Ingredients:
1 lb tender steak; Salt and pepper
3oz shredded suet;
1 small chopped onion;
1 lb shortcrust pastry

Tenderize the steak then cut it into narrow strips about an

inch long. Season to taste. Divide the pastry into three and roll each portion into an oval about ½ cm thick. Cover half of each pastry oval with meat to within about 2 cm of the edge. Sprinkle each bridie with its third of suet and onion, fold in two and press the edges together, between finger and thumb. Cut a small hole in each bridie and bake in a hot oven (230 C, Gas 7–8) till the pastry rises, then lower to moderate (180 C, Gas 3–4) for about an hour, until steak is tender.

While on gastronomic topics the _Glamis Cook Book_ ends with a recipe I rather liked, a 'recipe for Preserving Children', for which one needs '1 grassy field, 1 brook, some puppies (if available), some pebbles, 1½ dozen children (or more).

'Take the field and pour into it the children and dogs, allowing to mix well. Pour brook onto pebbles till slightly frothy. When children are nicely brown, cool in a warm bath. When dry serve with milk and fresh baked ginger bread.'

The whole village is old and unspoilt. One cottage still has a thatched roof and the old market cross still exists. After checking-in to be free of rucksacks and having some food the afternoon can go in making two visits.

Glamis folk museum

This is one of the best museums of its kind in the country, open May–September, noon–5.00pm. (Tel: 030 784 288). A long row of workers' cottages, looking very smart outside, have been linked cleverly inside so one walks the whole length of the buildings looking, in turn, at rooms displaying an old schoolroom, a chemist's shop, a weaver's room (you may get a demonstration) and various rooms in period houses. Across the road there is an additional display of agricultural machinery. The staff are helpful and knowledgeable. Children, up to the age of 99, find it fascinating. (National Trust for Scotland.)

Glamis Castle

The castle is open, May–Sept, afternoons only, Sunday to Friday (closed Saturday). Tel: 030 784 242.

Glamis Castle is an interesting contrast to Blair Castle. One enters by a big gateway and an even longer tree-lined avenue (mostly oak). A big 'doocot' lies to the left. Before the castle are statues of James I and Charles I, off right a unique many-faceted sundial — all that remains of numerous outer defences and gardens which were swept away in the 1770s when Capability Brown's parkland theories were paramount. The castle is of red sandstone, tall and turreted, as against Blair's white harling and solid building. Both have a long and turbulent history.

The connection with Macbeth and the witches is largely fiction but Malcolm II (the father of Duncan, Macbeth's victim) died in the castle after being wounded in battle nearby. Joanne, daughter of the first Stewart king, Robert II, married Sir John Lyon so the royal connection is an old one. Queen Elizabeth, the Queen Mother, reversed the order: as Elizabeth Bowes Lyon, she married the future King George VI. The sixth Lord Glamis had married a Douglas and James V in his paranoic hatred of the Douglases first imprisoned Lady Glamis and then had her burnt alive outside Edinburgh Castle. Even her son was condemned to death but he was released when the king died. He returned to a castle plundered by the king. Oddly James V's daughter visited Glamis but then, Mary Queen of Scots seems to have stayed everywhere!

The titles Earl of Kinghorne and the Earl of Strathmore and Kinghorne came in the next century. The second Earl beggared himself through his friendship with Montrose for when the latter deserted his Covenanting stand the earl poured everything he had into the Covenanters' cause. His son inherited an astronomical debt of £400,000 and somehow managed not only to survive but to thrive. The Old Pretender visited the castle — and his son was to stay at Blair Castle.

To Arbroath

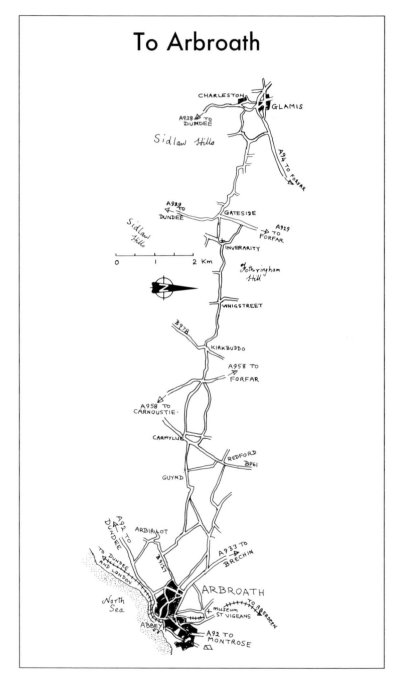

Day 14

On to the coast, Arbroath

OS54

The last day is entirely on roads but very minor ones and, of all the dozen or so similar lines I've made between hills and coast, this is the one I've most enjoyed. In late May 1988, on the last day of the Ultimate Challenge, no more than a dozen vehicles passed us all day. The scenery is pleasant throughout — a satisfying end to our varied coast-to-coast walk.

Leave Glamis by the A928 but once up under Hunters Hill take the path off it, left, to walk through the woods by a reservoir whose overflow's noise is as cheery as a waterfall's. If starting from Charleston take the path down through the trees from the top of the village, turn left for

---

Charleston, above Glamis — the start of the last day's walk.

Striding out through the coastal farmlands between Glamis and Arbroath.

Inverarity Church, one of several rural churches on the last day's route.

30 m, and the path to the reservoir is across the road. Watch out for the morning's Dundee commuters on this short bit of A road. The wood is largely beech and the walk up through the 'den' reminds me of beech forests in Corsica. At one place the path appears blocked by a barbed wire fence but double back behind this to continue on up to a gate onto the small road that circles Hunters Hill.

At Nether Airniefoul a small road goes off right, marked 'No through road'; this is _not_ the way to go. Turn left and on up to the highest point on the road. Just round a bend we turn off, right, to skirt along under the last swellings of the Sidlaw Hills, making for Gateside which now cringes below the striding, strident A929 Dundee–Aberdeen road. Forfar can be glimpsed to the north and the valley across to Fothringham Hill is rich agricultural land. Kincaldrum House is a sad ruin. Gateside is just a tidy hamlet; note the decorations above the doors on the gable facing the road. After passing under the A929 there is a 1 km straight to Inverarity, another small hamlet, where the grass by the banks between old and new bridges proved too great a temptation to our UC88 gang: we stopped there to brew tea — to the amusement of the tiny tots in the playground above our picnic spot.

The mill is really a big farm and the church is very attractive both in itself and its setting. Just beyond the church we come to the B9127 and turn right onto this road, which we follow all the way to Arbroath. At Whigstreet crossroads we meet the first signposting of the finish: 'Arbroath 11'.

In the wood to the east a Roman camp is shown on the map and if you keep an eye open for the farm track from Holemill coming in on the right you will be able to pin-point the site and see the remaining walls and ditches, cut by the road itself. Just before Kirkbuddo House a prehistoric cairn sits up on a bank to the right of our route. The woods here are completely covered with purslane: a sea of white and pink. (The first purslane we saw was yesterday, on the road before Kilry Church.) After Kirkbuddo House the B9127 steadily loses height, almost imperceptibly, as it heads eastwards. The farm name 'Curleys' rather caught our fancy but there are plenty of odd names along the road; see if you can spot Ovenstone, Goats, Dusty Drum, Gallow Hill, Wreaths, Drumyellow, Lochaber or Carrot ...

Tramping out the last mile of a coast-to-coast walk; two septuagenarians finishing in fine fettle.

Long straight sections and lesser views rather increase the psychological miles so another picnic is probably due. Stronger walkers may like to divert from Milton of Carmyllie 2 km to Redford, where the first building on the left on arrival is 'The Byre Restaurant' with good home produce. Forfar bridies should not be left unsampled. After passing the Guynd policies the road twists over the Elliot Water and for several miles parallels the course of an old railway. You will find great difficulty tracing any of it on the ground so intensely has the line been incorporated as farmland. There is a left turn at a T-junction (right goes to Arbirlot) and a last straight to the start of Arbroath. From the '30' speed restriction sign we had better have more detailed directions. The end is to be aesthetic — not just the quickest down to the rather barren, messed-up southern part of Arbroath's shoreline.

At the '30' sign, then, turn right onto Arbirlot Road West

The harbour at Arbroath — the East Coast at last.

which curves round to a T-junction with the Westway. Turn right and then, almost at once, left, onto Arbirlot Road. Follow this to its end (Keptie Road) and turn right along beside the park and its boating pond. Keep on in the same line: Nolt Loan Road is only indicated as one reaches a 'STOP' sign. Cross and continue on, along Alexandra Place (the name is up on a house, left), crossing the railway and with the sea visible beyond the war memorial in a park to the right of the road. Our road swings left and down to join another road, which we take leftwards. Turn off down East Mary Street, the first on the right, and this leads down to the dual carriageway of the A92 coast road, across which lies the harbour. The journey is over.

On the way down from the boating pond to the harbour several places offer B&B so you might be tempted to book in at once to be able to finish and explore without a pack. There is far too much to see really in what will be left of this day so

I'd suggest giving Arbroath a day to itself, a pleasant way to unwind and become re-absorbed into urban society again. Kintail and Loch Duich feels like another lifetime away.

If you have the energy, do walk around the harbour. It is a working port and fishing boats are still being built, there is a coastguard station, and several places still make the Arbroath smokey (smoked herring) which you can buy on the spot. Here too was the shore base for Stevenson's Bellrock lighthouse and the story of its construction and much else of local interest is told in the museum, which is in the Signal Tower, the 'lighthouse' just south of the harbour. Don't miss visiting the museum. There are rooms given over to the story of the Bellrock Lighthouse and local industries, fishing, wildlife, and the building itself is of historical interest. With no radio contact, the tower was built to make manual communication possible. Sometimes personal messages might be sent. Should the wife of a keeper give birth while her husband was on the rock, trousers or a petticoat hoisted aloft would convey the tidings! The Inchcape Reef or Bellrock lies 17 km out, in the mouth of the Tay and, being covered at high tide, had proved a menace for centuries. Tradition says the Abbot of Aberbrothock (Arbroath) placed a bell on the rock to warn shipping and this was removed by a wrecker who then ran into the reef himself. The story is told in the famous Southey poem. Robert Stevenson (grandfather of

Arbroath — a fishing boat under construction, a traditional craft that still survives today.

RLS) began the work of building a lighthouse in 1807 and it came into service in 1811. It is the oldest lit rock-tower still in use. The museum (0241 75598) is closed on Sundays.

Arbroath Abbey

The Abbey was founded in 1178 by King William the Lion who was buried there in 1214. It was consecrated in 1233. The layout was fairly standard and it must have been an impressive place, hard to envisage from the sad ruin of today. The Abbot's House alone has stood the ravages of time (at one time it was a thread factory) and now houses a small museum.

The Abbey however is famous for a parchment rather than any building. In 1320, after long years of battling for national survival and independence, the Scottish nobles met at Arbroath and, in a letter to the Pope, set out their feelings. The Declaration of Arbroath is one of the great statements of national rights. 'For, so long as a hundred remain alive, we will never in any degree be subject to the dominion of the English. Since not for glory, riches or honours do we fight, but for freedom alone, which no man loses but with his life.'

Such high declarations were seldom observed in practice. In 1446 the Lindsays took to arms in protest at yet another Ogilvy being appointed the Abbot's right-hand man. The

The Abbot's House, the best–preserved building in the Cathedral complex at Arbroath.

Abbey witnessed a savage battle on its doorstep when over 500 men were killed. That century saw the decline of genuine monasticism. The Abbots were place-seekers, worldly rather than spiritual, and documents show the monks living in a style far removed from the intended austerity. After Flodden (1513) there were plenty of ecclesiastical vacancies and a fifteen-year-old royal bastard became Arbroath's first lay Commendator. David Beaton gained Arbroath in 1524 and the notorious Cardinal's mistress, Mariot Ogilvy (mother of seven of his children) was granted part of its lands, and his nephew received Arbroath a few weeks before he was assassinated. The pious origins were not restored at the Reformation. Whoever was strong enough simply grabbed its title and wealth. The disgraced Hamilton or the king's favourite, Lennox, were typical. Dissolved and turned into a lordship by James VI, Arbroath was granted to Hamilton, now back in favour and created a marquis.

The Abbey simply fell into decay. The Abbot's House became a secular dwelling (so survived) but much else was left to crumble or was carted away as building stone for the town. When Dr Johnson visited the Abbey in 1773 he found only ruins 'to afford testimony of its ancient magnificence'. It is a strangely atmospheric place, even if the glory has departed.

Arbroath Cliffs' nature trail

For 9 km north of Arbroath there is spectacular old red sandstone cliff scenery, then the vast sands of Lunan Bay bite into the tiered, red coastline. The scale and quality of the cliff scenery and its wildlife come as quite a surprise. As a teenager already familiar with much of Scotland I can still recall the shock of discovery when I battled my way on a bike to Auchmithie youth hostel (long closed) and walked along the cliffs. As there is a good booklet I'll just tempt you with some of the names: The Needle E'e, The Mermaid's Kirk, Seaman's Grave, The Crusie, Deil's Heid, The Three Sisters, Dark Cave. The trail starts at Whiting Head at the end of the Promenade and is about 5 km in length. The cliffs can be followed for another 2 km to Auchmithie, 7 km by road, with a few buses on week days. Another alternative is to walk up

Seaton Den from Carlingheugh Bay to the Auchmithie road. Instead of walking back into town, cross the A9 westwards to St Vigeans where there is a museum with another collection of Pictish symbol stones. Meigle and St Vigeans alone have such displays. There are interesting gravestones in the church opposite the museum, with trades like weaving and fishing indicated on some of the stones.

Accommodation: Arbroath

Arbroath is a sizeable town with a wide range of accommodation (the official list names thirty places) and if need be the tourist office (open all year) can help: Angus Tourist Board, Market Place, Arbroath, DD11 1HR. 0241 72609/76680.

Camping Seaton Caravan and Camping Site, Seaton, by Arbroath. 0241 74762. On the northern outskirts of Arbroath in the grounds of an estate.

Reading HMSO: _Arbroath Abbey_ (this and other titles below are available on site or at museum).
Scottish Wildlife Trust: _Arbroath Cliffs Nature Trail_, 1971 and reprints since.
Libraries and Museum Services: _The Signal Tower; Illustrated Guide_.

Travel home

Bus station: Catherine Street, Arbroath. 0241 70646.
British Rail: 0241 73067.
Brown's taxis: 39 High Street, Arbroath. 0241 74234.
Trains on the Aberdeen–Edinburgh–London railway line stop at Arbroath so journeying home is very easy. Aberdeen–Dundee is a popular bus route and others travel Aberdeen–Edinburgh–London. One reason Arbroath was chosen as the finishing point was the ease with which one could leave it! And if that sounds bad, the leaving certainly is. One's heart is left in the hills and the journey home is made with very mixed feelings. The rucksack will be emptier but the memory stocked with goodies to last a lifetime.

*Arbroath: The Signal Tower (now an interesting museum) —
symbol of the finish.*

Appendix 1

Updating of information

There is always a continuous changing of the practical information concerning B&Bs, timetables, state of paths, opening hours of castles, shops, museums and so on. While the information in this guide is as comprehensive and accurate as possible there will be changes which will invalidate points of detail: a B&B may close, or a very useful bunkhouse open. To assist those planning a crossing I've made an Information Sheet which will be updated each year. The usefulness of this is obvious but to be as thorough as possible could I ask those who have made a crossing to report *any* changes they have encountered, so the information can be passed on. This will be sifted in the autumn and the updated Information Sheet available for early December, ready for the Christmas holiday dreaming of next summer's activities!

To obtain a copy please enclose a SAE and ten second class postage stamps: send to Scottish Mountain Holidays, C to C, 21 Carlin Craig, Kinghorn, Fife, KY3 9RX.

Appendix 2

Kit list

Murray's *Handbook* (1894) hints 'Even Alpine climbers need not despise several of the Scottish mountains' and makes various suggestions as to what should be carried: compass, field glass and a 'comforter of Shetland wool' (to be worn as a waistcoat or round the throat). 'A fair supply of provisions and a flask of Scotch whisky are among the indispensables.' And because of the dour manners of the Scots 'They should recollect that the Scottish middle and lower classes are not, as a rule, given to joking, except with their own dry, sententious humour.' The Scots, on that score, no doubt deserve their climate. 'Be prepared for every kind of weather, and gifted with a considerable stock of patience.'

Essentials	**Optionals** (seasonal or personal needs)
Set of day clothes, boots	Camera and film, etc
Waterproof top/bottom	Binoculars
Spare clothing	Logbook/writing materials
Maps and compass	Leisure reading
Whistle, small torch	Gaiters
First aid kit	Umbrella
Day rations	Short trousers
Rucksack	Gloves
Bivvy bag	Midge repellent
Money/cheque book, etc	Youth hostel card
Return travel tickets	Needle and thread/wool

Essentials
Change of clothing for evenings
Change of footwear for evenings
Minimal toilet needs
Small towel
Stove and pan, matches
Emergency rations
Some toilet paper
Spoon, pocket knife
Watch/alarm
Rain/sun hat
Pullover or such

Optionals
Suncream/dark glasses

Dogs, properly controlled, are all right on day walks but not on a coast to coast.

Appendix 3

Country code

Before you go
Ensure competence in map and compass work
Plan within your capabilities
Learn something of elementary First Aid
Know the Mountain distress signal
Check the weather forecast
Ensure adequate waterproofs and emergency gear are packed
Leave word of your route
Have day rations and extras prepared
If snow is likely to be encountered take ice axe and crampons
If weather is really bad modify plans (or postpone going)

When you go
Leave gates fastened
Don't climb walls: use gates
Guard against all risk of fire
Leave livestock, crops and machinery alone
Don't drop litter
Do not collect birds' eggs or plants
Progress quietly and wear unobtrusive clothing — and you'll see far more wildlife

Remember: not all this route is on rights-of-way and our presence is tolerated through the goodwill of landowners and the tenants on the land. While we have great freedom to roam in Scotland, it is a freedom based on mutual tolerance and co-operation. Respect what is, after all, the livelihood of the local population. Keep to the tracks in the stalking season and, if in doubt, *ask*. The natives are friendly!

Appendix 4

General bibliography

This is a very personal selection of books which I have found of interest in a life of walking the Scottish Highlands, so I trust they will interest others as well. It is a very brief selection but as well as the better general works I have added titles which may be of interest to a theme or a subject: forestry, history, sheep, mountain flowers, hydro works, castles for instance. Many titles are classics and will still be around in modern editions or paperbacks. Some may no longer be available through your local bookseller but all should be traceable through your local library. Some of the more local booklets mentioned in the text may only be found on the spot, so keep an eye open for them. Nevisport in Fort William has a big selection of books but Blair Castle, the NTS Visitor Centre in Killiecrankie, Pitlochry, and Arbroath are the only other places with a worthwhile selection of books.

Barnett, Ratcliffe: *The Road to Rannoch and the Summer Isles*, Grant, 1944.

Barrington, J.: *Red Sky at Night*, Michael Joseph, 1984 (in paperback now. The story of a shepherd's year in the Highlands).

Bartholomew: *Walk Perthshire*, 1986 (Bartholomew map and guide to 45 walks in Perth and Kinross District).

Barton, B. & Wright, B.: *A Chance in a Million — Scottish Avalanches*, Scottish Mountaineering Trust, 1985.

Bell, J. H. B.: *Bell's Scottish Climbs*, Gollancz, 1987 (reprint of a classic work).

Bennet, D. (ed.): *The Munros*, Scottish Mountaineering Club, 1985. *Ski Mountaineering in Scotland*, Scottish Mountaineering Club, 1988.

Bord, J. & C.: *Sacred Waters*, Granada, 1985 (Wells).

Borthwick, A.: *Always a Little Further*, Faber, 1939 (amusing, many reprints).

Brooker, W. (ed.): *A Century of Scottish Mountaineering*, 1988 (articles from 100 years of the Scottish Mountaineering Club Journal).

Brown, H. M.: *Climbing the Corbetts*, Gollancz, 1988. *Hamish's Mountain Walk*, Gollancz/Granada, 1980. *Travels*, Scotsman/GRF Sutherland, 1986. *The Great Walking Adventure*, Oxford Illustrated Press, 1986.

Butterfield, I.: *The High Mountains of Britain and Ireland*, Diadem, 1971.

Darling, F. F. & Boyd, J. M.: *The Highlands and Islands*, Collins/Fontana, 1965 (classic work on ecology).

Gordon, Seton: *Highways and Byways in the West Highlands*, 1935. *Highways and Byways in the Central Highlands*, 1949.

Grant, I. F.: *Highland Folk Ways*, Routledge and Kegan Paul, 1961.

Grimble, I.: *Highland Man*, Highlands & Islands Development Board, 1980 (one of an excellent series, all worth having).

Haldane, A. R. B.: *The Drove Roads of Scotland*, David & Charles, 1973 (authoritative and readable). *New Ways Through the Glens*, Nelson, 1962 (Telford, Mitchell etc).

Hart-Davis, D.: *Monarchs of the Glen*, Cape, 1978 (history of stalking).

Holden, A. E.: *Plant Life in the Scottish Highlands*, Oliver & Boyd, 1952.

Keay, J.: *Highland Drove*, Murray, 1984 (re-enacting of droving days).

Langmuir, E.: *Mountaincraft and Leadership*, Mountain Leadership Training Board, 1985 (the best hillwalkers' manual).

Lindsay, M.: *The Eye is Delighted*, Muller, 1971 (19th-century travellers' accounts). *The Discovery of Scotland*, Hale, 1964 (early travellers in Scotland).

MacCulloch, D. B.: *Romantic Lochaber, Arisaig and Morar*, Chambers, 1971.

MacNally, L.: *Highland Year, Wild Highlands, Highland Deer Forest*, Dent, 1968, 1970, 1972 (a keeper's experiences).

Moran, M.: *The Munros in Winter*, David & Charles, 1986. *Scotland's Winter Mountains*, David & Charles, 1988 (narrative and instruction).

Munro, N.: *The New Road*, Blackwood, 1914. *John Splendid*, Blackwood, 1898 (historical novels).

Murray, W. H.: *The Companion Guide to the West Highlands of Scotland*, Collins, 1968. *Scotland's Mountains*, Scottish Mountaineering Club, 1987 (a general survey).

Nethersole-Thompson, D.: *Highland Birds*, Highlands & Islands Development Board.

Nicolaisen, W. F. H.: *Scottish Place Names*, Batsford, 1976.

Pearsall, W. H.: *Mountains and Moorlands*, Collins New Naturalist, 1950.

Prebble, J.: *Culloden*, Secker/Penguin, 1961. *The Highland Clearances*, Penguin, 1963 (readable accounts of major episodes of Highland history).

Price, R. J.: *Highland Landforms*, Highlands & Islands Development Board, 1976.

Ratcliffe, D.: *Highland Flora*, Highlands & Islands Development Board, 1973.

Raven, J. & Walter, M.: *Mountain Flowers*, Collins New Naturalist, 1956.

Scottish Mountaineering Club District Guide series: the Western *Highlands*, *Central Highlands*, *Cairngorms* volumes cover this route. Very comprehensive & periodically updated.

Sissons, J. B.: *The Evolution of Scotland's Scenery*, Oliver & Boyd, 1967.

Stephen, D.: *Highland Animals*, Highlands & Islands Development Board, 1974.

Steven, Campbell R.: *The Story of Scotland's Hills*, Hale, 1975 (historical). *Glens and Straths of Scotland*, Hale, 1970.

Steven, H. M. & Carlisle, A.: *The Native Pine Woods of Scotland*, Oliver and Boyd, 1959.

Stott, L.: *The Waterfalls of Scotland*, Aberdeen University Press, 1987 (a profusely illustrated gazetteer).

Taylor, W.: *The Military Roads of Scotland*, David & Charles, 1976.

Thom, V. M.: *Birds in Scotland*, Poyser, 1986 (comprehensive survey).

Thomson, I. R.: *Isolation Shepherd*, Bidean Books, 1983 (now in paperback: remote Highland life).

Townsend, C.: *The Great Backpacking Adventure*, Oxford Illustrated Press, 1988 (ideas for future trips!).

Tranter, N.: *The Queen's Scotland: The Eastern Counties*, Hodder & Stoughton, 1972. *The Queen's Scotland: The Heartland*, Hodder & Stoughton, 1971 (excellent gazetteers).

Walker, B. & Ritchie, G.: *Exploring Scotland's Heritage: Fife & Tayside*, HMSO (one of eight volumes covering Scotland's best sites).

Weir, T.: *Highland Days*, Cassell, 1949 (Wright, 1986).

Wilson K. & Gilbert, R.: *The Big Walks*, *Classic Walks*, *Wild Walks*, Diadem, 1980, 1982, 1988 (glossy route descriptions).

Index

224